C000047858

Books are to be returned on or before
the last date below.

2 7 FEB 2010

2 5 MAR 2010

LIBREX–

International Finance Corporation
Washington, D.C.
2005

amazon | 13.95
Feb 2010
Pupil | Economics

© 2005 International Finance Corporation
2121 Pennsylvania Ave., N.W.
Washington, D.C. 20433
Telephone: 202-473-3800
Internet: www.ifc.org

All rights reserved

1 2 3 4 5 07 06 05

The findings, interpretations, and conclusions expressed herein are those
of the author(s) and do not necessarily reflect the views of the Board of
Directors of the International Finance Corporation or the governments they
represent.

The International Finance Corporation, part of the World Bank Group, does
not guarantee the accuracy of the data included in this work. The boundaries,
colors, denominations, and other information shown on any map in this work
do not imply any judgment on the part of the International Finance Corporation
or the World Bank concerning the legal status of any territory or the
endorsement or acceptance of such boundaries.

Rights and Permissions
The material in this publication is copyrighted. Copying and/or transmitting
portions or all of this work without permission may be a violation of applicable
law. The International Finance Corporation encourages dissemination of its
work and will normally grant permission to reproduce portions of the work
promptly.

For permission to photocopy or reprint any part of this work, please send a
request with complete information to the Copyright Clearance Center Inc.,
222 Rosewood Drive, Danvers, MA 01923, USA; telephone: 978-750-8400;
fax: 978-750-4470; Internet: www.copyright.com.

All other queries on rights and licenses, including subsidiary rights, should be
addressed to Corporate Relations, International Finance Corporation, 2121
Pennsylvania Avenue, N.W., Washington, DC 20433, USA; fax: 202-974-4384.

ISBN 0-8213-6228-3 978-0-8213-6228-3

eIISBN 0-8213-6229-1

DOI 10.1596/978-0-8213-6228-3

Copyright 2005 International Finance Corporation

All rights reserved
Manufactured in the United States of America
First printing June 2005

Library of Congress Cataloging-in-Publication data have been applied for.

Contents

Acknowledgments

This book is based on articles published by the World Bank's Rapid Response Unit (http://rru.worldbank.org/) and edited by Suzanne Smith. Some of the chapters were cowritten with colleagues at the World Bank Group: Bita Hadjimichael, Facundo Martin, Tatiana Nenova, and Klaus Tilmes. We are grateful to them.

Yogita Mumssen of the Global Partnership on Output-Based Aid wrote chapter 12. She would like to acknowledge the help of Luiz Tavares.

For insightful comments, or for advice or assistance, we would also like to thank Andy Berg, François Bourguignon, Mansoor Dailami, Simeon Djankov, Shahrokh Fardoust, Alan Gelb, Benjamin Herzberg, Pierre Jacquet, Philip Keefer, Steve Knack, Aart Kraay, Toshiya Masuoka, Mark McGillivray, Marta Reynal-Querol, David Roodman, Simon Scott, Warrick Smith, Mark Sundberg, and Bruno Wenn.

Most of all, we wish to thank Suzanne Smith for her patience, perceptiveness, and unflagging commitment to clear writing.

Introdu

1

The Market for Aid

If there is a market for aid, it is a strange one. Official aid agencies lament the fragmentation of their industry, but critics speak of a "cartel." Can both be right? In normal markets competition is good news because it increases efficiency, promotes innovation, and gives customers a better deal. Few people believe the market for aid works like this, but is there some reason why it cannot? Our aim in this book is to answer such questions by presenting the facts about the market for aid quickly and simply and showing what these facts mean for the aid industry and for the poor people the industry is supposed to be helping.

We are not shy in disclosing our enthusiasm for competitive markets. So we might be expected to be enthusiastic about the fact that the aid industry is growing ever more diverse and ever less concentrated. New aid agencies are always being set up; old ones are never shut down.

Yet our enthusiasm is guarded, for three reasons. The first is that competition between aid agencies has real costs. Among recipient governments the weaker or less public-spirited ones may be tempted to overstretch themselves and accept too many small projects at too high a cost in time and scarce civil service expertise. It is nice to enjoy a choice of 10 cafes, but not if you must buy a tenth of a cappuccino at each.

The second reason is that competition is often distorted—for example, by poorly disciplined subsidies. An aid agency that hands out cheap loans carelessly may succeed in doing nothing more than destroying the commercial loan industry.

The third and most important reason is that the market for aid does not always produce enough information to allow meaningful choices by recipients and donors. We have a weak grasp of what kind of aid really works. The book sets out what we know about the performance of different types of donors and the effectiveness of different types of aid, but we have to conclude that our knowledge is still rudimentary.

The aid industry remains keen on "harmonization," an attempt to reduce the costs of competition by, for example, eliminating duplication of donor efforts. This attempt is laudable, but since the entry of new aid agencies will surely continue, the harmonization agenda has its limits. We argue that competition has already had benefits for the poor and that with determined efforts those benefits can be multiplied many times.

Competition in the market for aid is increasing, but it is not yet intense. The typical recipient country faces a concentrated aid industry—equivalent to three equally sized donors, according to the most widely used measure of market concentration. In the United States such a triopoly would merit an investigation from the Federal Trade Commission; talk of uncontrollable fragmentation goes too far.

Still, aid agencies face competition not only from one another but from the private sector. For example, many countries can take competitively priced loans from private banks or the bond markets rather than aid agencies. That the typical developing country is borrowing more from multilaterals—while still reducing debt levels—tells us that the aid industry is providing a valuable service in the face of real competition and that many if not most recipients are using that service sensibly. The true value of private sector finance is not as a substitute for official aid but as a new and complementary product. Remittances from migrant workers, for example, are now a large source of funds, especially for people in the poorest countries. They are something new, exciting, and maybe even better than official aid, but they certainly do not render it obsolete.

Remittances to households and loans to private companies can only strengthen the private sector in developing countries, and there is no doubt that private enterprise can survive in the most unpromising environments (as chapter 11, on Somalia, shows). The official aid industry can help by encouraging governments to improve their investment climates and encouraging private firms to act in ways that not only will be profitable but will help the poor. There is rich scope here for hybrid development banks—or for joint ventures between development banks—that provide loans, guarantees, and guidance to the private sector, advice to governments, and well-targeted grants to the poor.

One benefit of competition in the market for aid is that it can give us a better sense of which financial flows best help the poor. So far researchers on aid effectiveness have scarcely asked this question, confining themselves to asking where aid should be sent rather than how it should be sent, what it should be used for, and how other financial flows compare with aid flows.

This is a serious gap in our knowledge. What little we do know is worrying: Aid may have a harmful effect on the governance of recipient countries. And grants, an increasingly popular way to give aid, historically have not seemed to encourage investment or economic growth. We are optimists on these points and believe that aid can be given without damaging governance and that grants can be given that boost investment and economic growth. But we are not so optimistic as to think that this will happen purely by accident.

The aid industry needs to make its own luck, innovating by experimenting widely and evaluating the results of those experiments much more rigorously than in the past. Experimentation is probably an automatic side effect of a diverse industry. But without credible tests, that experimentation will not tell us what we need to know to improve aid projects. The industry is far behind the medical profession, which has used randomized trials to evaluate medical treatments for more than half a century. Such trials can be and have been used to evaluate development projects, without incurring heavy expense—but nongovernmental organizations, not the official aid agencies, have been at the forefront of this research. That is a shame.

Our final chapters speculate on two possible scenarios for the future of the aid industry. Scenarios are not predictions or forecasts but stories that provoke useful questions, the most useful being, What would we do if this happened?

In one scenario, the *Rise of the Undergrowth*, the official aid industry is sidetracked by political concerns. This is nothing new, since geopolitics has always been an important part of foreign aid. What is new in this scenario is that so many alternatives are available. Remittances, charitable giving, and commercial money flood into developing countries, along with cheap and efficient systems for monitoring results—and nobody misses the official aid industry.

In the other scenario, the *Big Push*, we explore a possible future for well-meaning harmonization efforts. Because of a lack of innovation and a lack of knowledge about what works well, initial results are disappointing. The industry keeps learning and changing, however, and eventually a form of competition within a harmonized framework delivers results for the poor.

Neither of these scenarios will unfold exactly as described, though they highlight important trends. But we are sure of one thing: if the official aid industry tries to shut down competition, it will fail. The market for aid will continue to become increasingly diverse and complex, with more players, more options, and more demands. If aid agencies can harness that diversity to meet those demands, the opportunities for the poor people we are supposed to be helping will be rich indeed.

PART II

Understanding the Market for Aid

2

Aid Agency Competition

A Century of Entry, but No Exit

Critics of the aid industry have accused it of acting like a cartel (Easterly 2002). The accusation has some bite—globally the industry remains somewhat concentrated, and for the typical recipient country, highly concentrated. Yet the most striking fact about the industry is how relentlessly competitive pressures are building. There has been a constant stream of new entrants, a steady fall in global and local concentration, and a clear tendency for donors to break out of historical patterns of aid and compete with one another. Could greater competition improve the efficiency of the aid system?

The postwar wave of modern aid agencies included the U.S. Agency for International Development (USAID), some export credit agencies, and the Bretton Woods institutions, all in response to the world's needs after World War II (figure 1).

The second wave, arriving between 1955 and 1980, had a different character. True, the World Bank agencies established—the International Development Association (IDA) and the International Finance Corporation (IFC)—were apparently a response to previously unmet needs. But many of the other agencies seemed to appear because there was money to spare rather than in response to a change in the world's needs. The new agencies included Japan's huge Overseas Economic Cooperation Fund (OECF), the regional development banks in booming Europe and Asia, and several agencies funded by oil windfalls.

Entry to the market is continuing as new agencies find new business models—or new recipient countries, in the case of the European Bank

Figure 1 The aid century

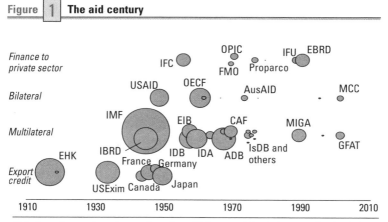

Note: Agencies are shown in year of creation, with the area of the circles proportional to their most recent annual aid commitments in U.S. dollars. ADB is Asian Development Bank; CAF, Corporación Andina de Fomento; EHK, Euler Hermes Kreditversicherungs; EIB, European Investment Bank; FMO, Netherlands Development Finance Company; IDB, Inter-American Development Bank; IMF, International Monetary Fund; and OPIC, Overseas Private Investment Corporation. *IsDB and others* includes the Islamic Development Bank, the OPEC Fund, and the Arab Monetary Fund. For others, please see the text. Some organizations with annual commitments less than US$1.75 million are not labeled.
Source: OECD Development Assistance Committee; authors' compilation.

for Reconstruction and Development (EBRD). EBRD serves private sector clients, as do its large contemporary, the Multilateral Investment Guarantee Agency (MIGA), and France's Proparco and Denmark's Investment Fund for Central and Eastern Europe (IFU). Recently two new agencies—the Global Fund to Fight AIDS, Tuberculosis, and Malaria (GFAT) and the Millennium Challenge Corporation (MCC)—started operations. They are expected to expand quickly in the next two or three years. In addition, emerging economies such as China and Slovenia have moved to set up aid agencies. The prospects for continued innovation and new entry seem good. Despite this, there has been very little exit. All the agencies created since 1945 still exist.

How much has competition increased?

Even when studying a profit-making private industry it is not easy to measure the intensity of competition. But it is possible to track concentration, the measure of how much market share is in the hands of a few large players. Concentration is not perfectly correlated with a lack of competition but is highly suggestive of it.

Industrial economists measure concentration using the Herfindahl index, which ranges from 0 (perfect competition) to 1 (monopoly).[1] Under U.S. competition policy a Federal Trade Commission (FTC) investigation would regard an index of more than 0.18 as meaning "highly concentrated"—not proof of an uncompetitive industry but certainly reason to be suspicious.

Had the FTC been asked to investigate the international aid industry in the 1950s, it would have discovered an index of more than 0.5 (figure 2). At the time the aid industry was dominated by U.S. postwar aid flows. Now it has a Herfindahl index of around 0.1—"mildly concentrated" by FTC standards.

For comparison, figure 2 shows the range of concentration of primary commodities in the 1990s as estimated by Verleger (1993), with each producing country treated as a single entity. The range is from

---

1. The Herfindahl index is the sum of the squares of the market shares of industry players.

Figure 2 | **Competition grows in the aid industry**

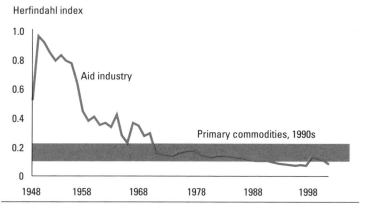

Herfindahl index

Source: OECD Development Assistance Committee; authors' calculations; Verleger 1993.

0.208 (rubber) to 0.085 (oil). Over the years the aid industry has moved from well above this range to near the bottom of it.

Competition between bilateral donors

Competition may take place between aid agencies but also between donor countries. The inherent competitiveness of the aid industry seems to be increasing on both levels, because besides establishing new agencies without closing down old ones, donor countries seem to be moving in on one another's "turf."

That bilateral donations show geographical patterns and historical persistence is well known. For example, France and the United Kingdom send aid to former colonies; Australia concentrates on Asia, Oceania, and the Pacific islands; and Japan's major beneficiaries are large East Asian economies. One effect of such patterns is to limit competition. Just as cartels always seek ways to divide up the market in a stable fashion, donors might stick to historical partners if they were attempting to suppress competition in the aid industry.

Yet the historical patterns are changing faster than in the past. Donors' lists of favorite recipients changed more in the 1990s than in the 1980s. For the major donors that make up the Development Assistance Committee (DAC) of the Organisation for Economic Co-operation and Development (OECD), only 5 new entrants made it to the list of the top 15 recipients in 1982–92, but 7 new entrants did in 1992–2002 (figure 3). The more rapidly shifting patterns of aid do not support the contention that aid is increasingly cartelized.

Donors are also spreading their aid more thinly across the world. For nearly three-quarters of donors (14 of the 19 DAC members for which data were available) the share of aid flowing to the region that received the most declined between 1982 and 2002. Thus the market is less segmented, allowing more opportunity for competition.

The corollary from the point of view of recipient countries is that they receive aid from more donors. The World Bank (2004, p. 172) recently published an index of donor fragmentation for recipient coun-

Figure 3 **Patterns of aid are shifting more quickly**

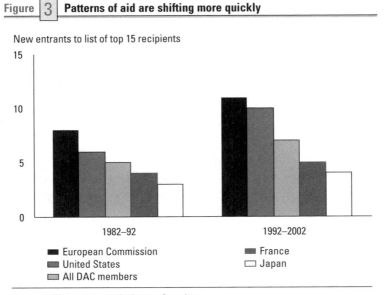

New entrants to list of top 15 recipients

Legend:
- European Commission
- United States
- All DAC members
- France
- Japan

Source: OECD Development Assistance Committee.

tries, which rose from an average of 56 in 1975 to 67 in 2002. But while fragmentation at the country level is rising, it is still quite low. An index of 56 would be produced by three donors alone, one providing 60 percent of aid flows and the other two 20 percent each. An index of 67 would be produced by three equal donors.

Impact on the World Bank Group

Multilateral aid agencies[2] have been winning market share from bilateral and export credit agencies for the past three decades, but the World Bank Group has been losing market share since the mid-1980s (figure 4). The International Bank for Reconstruction and Development (IBRD) was smaller in 2002 than in any year since 1985, even before adjusting for inflation.

Consequences and responses

In well-functioning markets an increase in competition is almost always good news for customers and bad news for incumbents. Almost everyone has abandoned the once widespread belief that competition is wasteful and that a centrally planned economy would do much better. We now realize that any "waste" generated by the competitive process is dwarfed by its ability to push firms to innovate, cut costs, and respond to customer demand.

But the aid system is at best a quasi-market. It is not always clear who the customers are. Thus for the aid industry it is not so ridiculous to say that competition is wasteful and should be managed. For example, Stephen Knack and Aminur Rahman (2004), constructing a model in which competing donors poach the best local government staff to run projects, find that donor fragmentation is associated with lower-quality bureaucracies in recipient countries.

The aid industry has attempted to limit these costs by calling for more cooperation. Such calls have become more prevalent as competi-

---

2. Including the World Bank Group, the United Nations, the regional development banks, and the European Commission.

Figure 4 Multilaterals grow in importance, but the World Bank Group shrinks

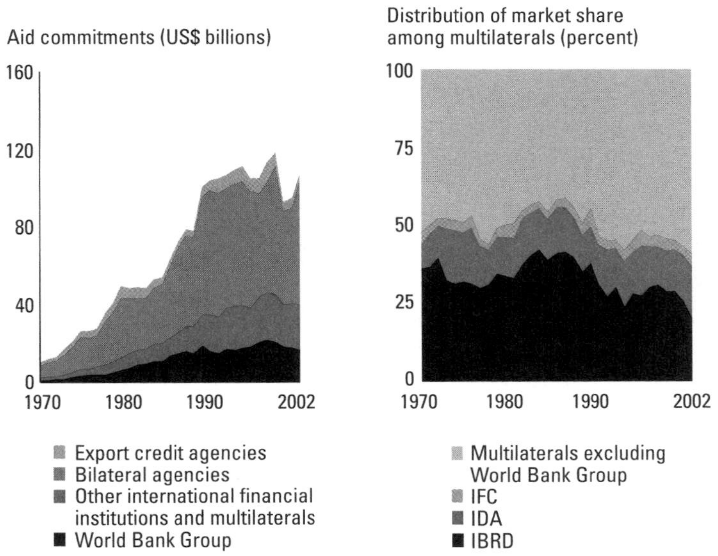
Aid commitments (US$ billions)
160
120
80
40
0
1970
1980
1990
2002
Export credit agencies
Bilateral agencies
Other international financial institutions and multilaterals
World Bank Group
Distribution of market share among multilaterals (percent)
100
75
50
25
0
1970
1980
1990
2002
Multilaterals excluding World Bank Group
IFC
IDA
IBRD

Source: OECD Development Assistance Committee.

tion has increased.[3] But can this response be sustained in the face of continued entry? Most cartels—whether predatory or altruistic—attract entry and are not resilient when it happens.

An alternative strategy is to embrace the increasing competitiveness of the aid "market" and use it to make the market work better. There is no reason that the agencies that set priorities and donate money need to be the agencies that use the money to deliver services. Should aid agencies "make aid" or simply "buy aid"? Since competition would probably be much more productive between service delivery organiza-

3. One way to get a sense of this trend is to survey the titles of papers presented to the Bank-Fund Development Committee since its founding in 1974. No titles mentioned *partnership*, *joint programs*, or *harmonization* before 1985, but 14 have since then, 10 of them in the past five years.

tions than between donor organizations, this split has some attractions. There are several ways in which it might happen:

- Effective outsourcing of aid to "execution agencies" would need to be based on better monitoring and benchmarking of agencies' performance. Donors would be able to achieve desired results more effectively if they knew which agencies deserved their money.

- Existing agencies could be split up to make such outsourcing easier. The Commonwealth Development Corporation in the United Kingdom was split into an agency that gives money and a government-owned limited liability company that delivers services. It is quite possible to conceive of a market for corporate control emerging between service delivery agencies, and for-profit companies freely entering the business.

- Going further, poor people could be given aid vouchers so they could purchase services directly, an idea floated by William Easterly (2002). Of course, both the economic and the political obstacles to this proposal are formidable.

The competitive pressures faced by aid agencies can be exaggerated, but they are real and growing. It is therefore worth exploring ways to turn this trend to the advantage of the poor. In the short term the most promising way to do so is to improve the monitoring and benchmarking of aid agencies, enabling donors to channel funds through the agencies that produce the best results.

The Demand for Loans

Governments Restructure Their Debt

More than ever, governments in developing countries have access to capital markets, but most are not using it. Instead, they have restructured their debt portfolios, cutting the share of private sector debt and increasing the share of longer-term multilateral debt. While some argue that this increase in official debt is alarming, the evidence suggests that most governments are sensibly taking advantage of their menu of financing options—extending maturities to lessen their vulnerability to the "rollover risk" posed by shorter-term debt and reducing their overall debt ratios.

The number of emerging markets rated by Moody's grew tenfold between 1986 and 1999, and the quality of ratings has also risen (figure 1). In broadening the countries rated, the rating agencies were both responding to the demand for ratings of emerging market sovereign bonds and fueling that demand: in the 1970s bank lending was nearly 20 times the bond issues for emerging markets, but by the 1990s bond issues had surpassed bank lending (Setty and Dodd 2003).

This increase in credit quality has been accompanied by extremely small spreads on private debt relative to debt from the aid industry or other official sources (see figure 1 and box 1). The improvement in average credit quality is simple enough to explain: developing countries reduced their debt burdens and adopted better policies. Median inflation rates, for example, after ranging above 10 percent for nearly a quarter of a century, fell below 5 percent in 1999 and so far have stayed there.

Yet the availability of cheap money has provoked no surge in indebtedness to private markets like those in the 1980s in many places, especially upper-middle-income countries. Since the late 1990s a much more modest boom has occurred in upper-middle-income countries, while borrowing from private sources by low-income countries has collapsed (see figure 1).

Away from private, toward multilateral debt

Middle-income countries have greatly reduced their debt burden relative to gross national income (GNI) since 1990, in part by paying off substantial official debt (figure 2). By contrast, low-income countries have preferred to borrow from official sources. In these countries private sector debt has been falling since the mid-1990s, from about 14 percent of GNI in 1994 to about 5 percent in 2002. Official finance continues to go to low-income borrowers, with the balance of official debt shifting away from bilateral lenders and toward multilaterals over the past 15 years. (Part of the explanation lies on the supply side: some bilateral lending operations have been wound up.)

Middle-income countries have also clearly shifted away from bilateral debt. For these countries around 60 percent of official debt is now

Figure 1 Emerging markets have seen their credit ratings rise in number and quality . . .

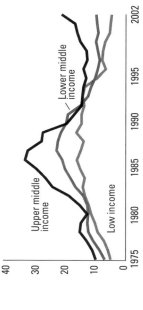

Number and quality of Moody's credit ratings for emerging markets

Average Standard & Poor's credit rating for emerging markets

. . . but despite the availability of cheap money have shown no recent surge in private market borrowing

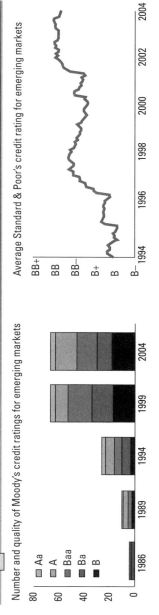

Spread between private and official debt for developing countries (basis points)

Private sector sovereign debt as a percentage of GNI

Note: Rating agencies use different scales. The Standard & Poor's BB+, BB, and BB− are comparable to the Moody's Ba. The Standard & Poor's B+, B, and B− are comparable to the Moody's B.

Source: For Moody's ratings, IMF 1999 and Moody's; for average credit ratings, IMF 2004; for all other data, World Bank, Global Development Finance database.

Box About the data

This chapter discusses three types of sovereign debt. *Bilateral debt* describes loans to governments from other governments or government agencies, including central banks and official export credit agencies. *Multilateral debt* is debt from the multilateral agencies, such as the World Bank or the regional development banks. Official debt is the sum of bilateral and multilateral debt. *Private sector sovereign debt* is credit extended by commercial banks, exporters, or suppliers of goods or raised from the bond market.

All graphs except the top two in figure 1 are based on data from the World Bank's Global Development Finance database. These graphs are limited to countries for which data are available back to 1975—typically 39 low-income countries, 26 lower-middle-income countries, and 14 upper-middle-income countries. These 79 countries produced 59 percent of developing country gross national income (GNI) in 2002. Key omissions include China, the Russian Federation, and the countries of Eastern Europe. Nevertheless, when graphs are redrawn as data become available for additional countries, most patterns are very similar.

from multilaterals, compared with around 35 percent in 1975. In lower-middle-income countries bilateral debt fell from about 45 percent of GNI in the early 1990s to about 18 percent in 2002. Multilateral debt fell much more modestly, from 25 percent of GNI to 19 percent.

Upper-middle-income countries have borrowed far less heavily, with a larger share of their debt (55 percent) from private sources. They too have restructured their official debt, borrowing less from bilaterals and more from multilaterals.

Thus bilateral debt has become less important relative to multilateral debt in all country income groups. As a share of total official debt, it fell from 71 percent in 1975 to 40 percent in 2002 in low-income countries, and from 70 percent to 45 percent in lower-middle-income countries. In upper-middle-income countries it fell from 63 percent to about 33 percent.

Figure 2 **A shift toward multilateral debt**

Low-income countries
Total sovereign debt as a percentage of GNI

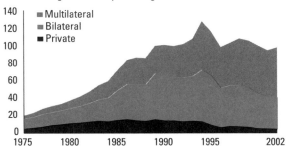

Lower-middle-income countries
Total sovereign debt as a percentage of GNI

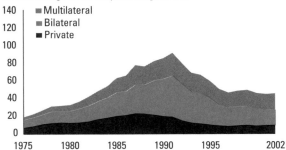

Upper-middle-income countries
Total sovereign debt as a percentage of GNI

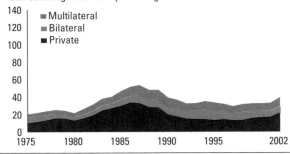

Source: World Bank, Global Development Finance database.

Who is lending?

Grouping countries by their recent level of indebtedness gives a similar picture of the composition of official debt: while bilateral debt added up to 65–70 percent of total official debt in 1975, it fell to about 47 percent in 2002 in severely indebted countries, 38 percent in moderately indebted countries, and 32 percent in less indebted ones.[1]

Multilateral debt rose from less than 5 percent of GNI in 1975 in severely and moderately indebted countries to about 44 percent in 2002 in severely indebted countries and 40 percent in moderately indebted ones. From a similar initial level, multilateral debt increased to about 18 percent of GNI in less indebted countries.

Official debt increased as a share of the total from the mid-1980s to the mid-1990s in all countries, regardless of indebtedness. It rose from 65 percent in 1983–84 to about 78 percent in 2002 in both severely and less indebted countries, following a similar trajectory in moderately indebted countries.

Multilaterals as lender of first resort?

The picture emerging is that despite declining spreads—and improving credit ratings for many countries—the typical developing country is shying away from borrowing on capital markets and shifting its debt portfolio toward official, especially multilateral, debt.

The chief attraction of official debt appears to be not its cost but its long maturities (figure 3). Official debt has an average maturity of more than 20 years, while private debt has one of around 10 years. For low-income countries, the most avid consumers of official debt, the maturity of official debt is around four times that of private debt.

The question is whether the shift toward multilateral debt is a positive trend or a worrying one. The pessimistic view is that countries are using overly generous loans from multilaterals to extend themselves

---

1. Countries are considered severely indebted if the present value of their debt service exceeds 80 percent of gross national income or 220 percent of exports, moderately indebted if one of these ratios is 60 percent or more of the level for severely indebted countries, and less indebted if these ratios are less than 60 percent of that level.

Figure 3 Long maturities are the chief attraction of official debt

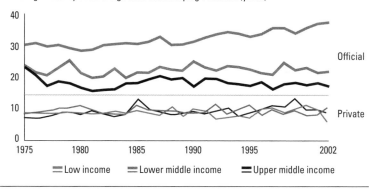

Average maturity of sovereign debt of developing countries (years)

Low income   Lower middle income   Upper middle income

Source: World Bank, Global Development Finance database.

too far, postponing (but increasing) the pain of readjustment and leaving the bill for future generations. The optimistic view is that countries are sensibly taking advantage of the financing menu offered them—extending maturities to lessen their vulnerability to the "rollover risk" posed by short-term debt and reducing their overall debt levels.

The evidence here supports cautious optimism. Upper-middle-income countries have modest debt, while lower-middle-income countries have reduced their debt consistently and substantially since the early 1990s. Low-income countries clearly remain vulnerable, but they have checked their accumulation of debt after two decades and even made modest steps toward reducing it. A possibility remains that indebtedness will move in the wrong direction, but the evidence suggests that developing countries are taking a rational approach in their demand for sovereign debt, with considerable help from the multilateral development banks. There have been frequent suggestions in recent years from nongovernmental organizations and some politicians that there should be no role for official loans in future; the evidence suggests that many countries are learning to use official loans and that the long maturities provided by these loans are a valuable option for the governments of developing countries.

Having said that, most finance for developing countries is no longer sovereign debt but nonsovereign debt or equity. Chapter 6 analyzes these trends in private flows.

4

The Supply of Aid

How Are Donors Giving, and to Whom?

This chapter reviews trends in official development assistance, focusing on volumes, sources, forms, and recipients. Several patterns emerge. First, a long-term trend of official flows taking the form of "hard" loans rather than grants and "soft" loans, with low interest and long maturities, has been reversed in the past five years. Second, both grants and loans are increasingly aimed at middle-income countries rather than the poorest. And third, official flows have fallen relative to rich-country income by 30 percent in the past 30 years.

The ever-shifting debate over the aid industry and the right way to help the world's poor has acquired new elements in recent years. There is a new, overdue, and welcome focus on measuring results. No longer is it enough to point, whether with pride or with criticism, at the raw volume of money transferred. New debates have surfaced.

Some of these debates center on how aid is delivered. Which is more important: better monitoring of aid projects or reducing the transaction costs of lending? Which kinds of recipients make the best use of aid: governments, nongovernmental organizations, companies, or individuals? What organizations give the most effective aid? And which form should aid take: grants, loans, or something else?

The new focus on results adds spice to a third trend: the continuing emergence of competition in the aid industry. Competition is forcing organizations to demonstrate that they can produce results.

But it is early days for the results agenda, and most hard data collection still focuses on raw flows. Those flows are not easy to interpret. Even a simple question such as whether aid is increasingly or decreasingly directed to the poor poses difficulties: the poor in 1970 were not where they are in 2004. Some countries that were once poor have grown quickly and are now classified as middle income. Yet many countries now classified as middle income still have huge numbers of poor people within their borders. Moreover, many new countries have been created, especially in the past 15 years.

Nevertheless, some trends are apparent:

- A long-term trend of more official finance being provided on nonconcessional terms has been reversed within the past five years.

- As a share of rich-country income, official development assistance (ODA) has shrunk by 30 percent since the 1970s.

- The multilateral agencies emphasized nonconcessional ("hard") loans until recently, but in the past few years these have declined.[1]

---

1. The analysis of multilateral flows here excludes the International Monetary Fund (IMF) because IMF funding is concerned mostly with financial stability and because data on IMF flows have not been consistently reported by members of the OECD Development Assistance Committee.

- Bilateral agencies generally give grants rather than loans.

- Concessional ("soft") loans make up a relatively small share of the funding from both bilateral and multilateral agencies.

- Low-income countries are receiving a diminishing share of grants, soft loans, and hard loans.

- Grants boomed after the collapse of the Soviet bloc but are no longer rising even in nominal terms (there has been an uptick very recently, and it is too early to judge whether this is a turning point or not).

Official aid effort is shrinking

Official flows of finance from rich to poor countries are smaller than they used to be, relative to the economies of the rich countries. Of the US$104 billion sent to poor countries in 2002, just under a third, US$34 billion, was "other official flows" (OOF)—meaning that it took the form of loans at or near market interest rates or was otherwise judged by the Development Assistance Committee of the Organisation for Economic Co-operation and Development (OECD) to lack a development purpose. The rest was ODA: grants or loans with generous payback periods and low interest rates. ODA slipped from around 80 percent of official flows in the 1970s to less than 60 percent in the late 1990s, but has recently recovered to more than 70 percent.

Since the 1970s the flows of grants and soft loans have shrunk by more than a quarter relative to the gross national income (GNI) of high-income OECD countries (figure 1). (This is a measure that donor watchers call aid effort.)

Growth in multilateral hard loans is reversed

The fastest growing sector of the official aid industry was until recently hard loans from multilateral aid agencies, but these have declined sharply in recent years (figure 2). Bilateral agencies, which give or lend money directly from one government to another, generally give grants rather than loans. Such grants have maintained their market share

Figure `1` **Official flows are shrinking**

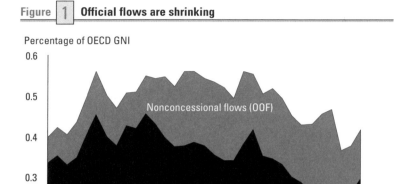

Percentage of OECD GNI

Source: OECD Development Assistance Committee.

since 1970. Over the past 30 years soft loans from bilateral agencies have lost ground to loans, both hard and soft, from multilateral agencies and hard loans from bilateral agencies.

Are poorer countries missing out?

The aggregate trend in aid seems to be a shift away from low-income countries and toward middle-income countries (figures 3 and 4).[2] This trend is most apparent for grants. In the 1970s around 70 percent of ODA grants went to low-income countries (figure 5). In the 1990s this share fell dramatically, to 50 percent.

The share of nonconcessional loans disbursed to low-income countries also fell—from 29 percent in the 1980s to 21 percent since 1990. Although bilateral agencies recently expanded nonconcessional lend-

---

2. All classifications by income are based on World Bank categories in 2004. So a fall in the share of aid to low-income countries indicates a fall in the share given to countries that are poor *today*. Since countries tend to graduate to middle-income status, this way of measuring understates the decline in aid to poor countries.

Figure 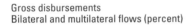 **Rise of bilateral grants—and rise and fall of multilateral loans**

Gross disbursements
Bilateral and multilateral flows (percent)

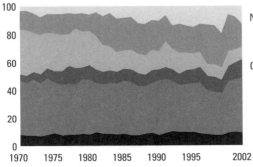

Nonconcessional (OOF)
  ▨ Bilateral loans
  ▨ Multilateral loans
Concessional (ODA)
  ▨ Bilateral loans
  ▪ Multilateral loans
  ▪ Bilateral grants
  ▪ Multilateral grants

Bilateral flows (US$ billions)

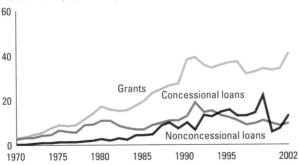

Multilateral flows (US$ billions)

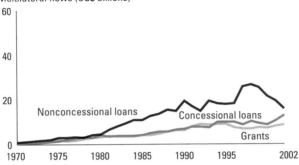

Source: OECD Development Assistance Committee.

Figure 3 **Grants aimed less at poor countries**

Gross disbursements by recipient country income group

Multilateral grants (percent)

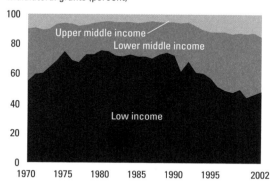

Bilateral grants (percent)

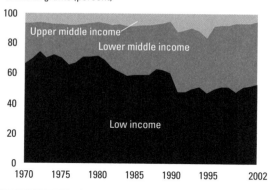

Source: OECD Development Assistance Committee.

ing to low-income countries, this growth is from a very low base and does little to offset the decline in multilateral lending to these countries.

Where will growth in aid come from?

The fall in the share of grants to low-income countries was driven largely by the boom in grants to Central and Eastern Europe following

Figure 4   **Nonconcessional loans aimed at middle-income countries**

Gross disbursements by recipient country income group

Multilateral loans (percent)

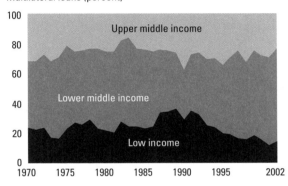

Bilateral loans (percent)

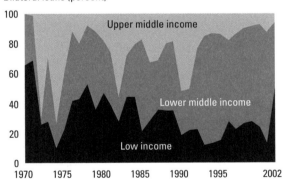

Source: OECD Development Assistance Committee.

the collapse of the Soviet bloc (figure 6). But without that boom, grants would look even more stagnant than they already do. This is part of a pattern of aid growth being driven by successive reconstruction and development booms. Such booms followed the end of World War II, the appearance of independent former colonies, and the collapse of communism.

Figure 5 Poor countries missing out on both grants and loans

Official gross disbursements to low-income countries as
a percentage of those to low- and middle-income countries

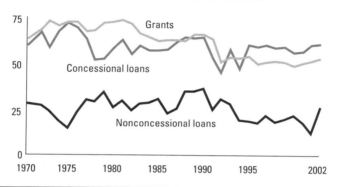

Source: OECD Development Assistance Committee.

Figure 6 Central and Eastern Europe and the grant boom

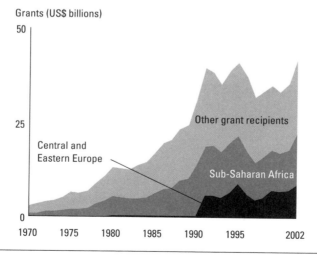

Source: OECD Development Assistance Committee.

Figure 7 Flows to the private sector outpace public sector flows

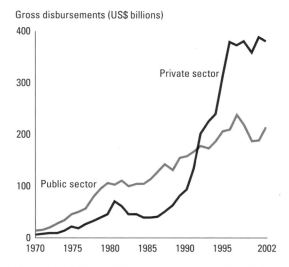

Gross disbursements (US$ billions)

Note: *Private sector* denotes nonguaranteed debt, grants by nongovernmental organizations, and workers' remittances, plus portfolio equity and direct investment, which are reported net. *Public sector* denotes gross disbursements from bilateral and multilateral agencies (including the International Monetary Fund), export credit guarantees, and private borrowing with a public guarantee.
Source: World Bank 2004.

Private finance is providing competition

The private sector is now hugely important as both a source and a recipient of loans and even grants. The complexity of the picture defies neat categorization, but figure 7 gives a general impression, comparing disparate sources of funding for the private sector with finance to or guaranteed by the public sector. Private sector lending to middle-income countries competes with loans from the development banks. Other private flows provide indirect competition. For example, workers' remittances exceed official grants in both low- and middle-income countries and are more stable than private investment and official aid. Chapters 3, 6, and 9 analyze the relationship between private and official flows in more depth.

5

Donor Performance

What Do We Know, and What Should We Know?

It would be hard to disagree with the objectives of the international aid industry. But how much are donors contributing to their achievement? Despite recent progress, we still know surprisingly little. We know that some donors give much more than others relative to income. We also know that donors are focusing aid less on poor countries and more on countries with strong institutions or good policies. And we know that there appears to be no tradeoff here: the countries that give the most aid also target poor countries and those with good policies. Yet we are still in the dark about which donors, or which projects, are achieving the best results.

Much commentary on the aid industry focuses purely on the volume of aid. While the size of aid flows matters, there is surely more to be said. Not all dollars of aid are equivalent; some help the poor, and some do not. Researchers are therefore paying growing attention to the quality of the aid given by donors (sometimes in an attempt to provoke better practices). But there is a problem: before measuring the average quality or effectiveness of aid, we need to know what makes aid high quality or effective. We have only a vague idea of this, and tentative early research has revealed little except the paucity of the data. As a result, researchers have tended to base their work on plausible assumptions rather than solid research.

What determines the effectiveness of aid?

Analysts of donor performance have variously made three types of assumption. The first is that aid does more good if it goes to poor countries. This is clearly plausible, holding other things equal. Yet there may be reasons that aid flowing to poor countries does not help the poor. Many poor people live in countries that are not themselves very poor. And poorer countries tend to have less ability to use aid effectively.

The second assumption, then, is that aid does more good if given to countries with good policies or good institutions. This claim is based on a widespread view that aid works well if the recipient country does the right things with it—thus the famous claim that "aid works in a good policy environment." The paper that kicked off the debate, Burnside and Dollar (2000), is too specific to support such a blanket claim. Burnside and Dollar use a narrow definition of "a good policy environment" (a particular combination of low inflation, fiscal rectitude, and an open economy) and "aid works" (GDP growth in the recipient country must be higher in the four-year period following the four-year period in which the aid was received). Subsequent analysis has shown that the conclusions change dramatically if the specification of the model is changed or the data set expanded. Nevertheless, since the basic idea that "good governments" use aid better than "bad governments" remains plausible, it seems right that it should play a role in evaluating aid quality.

The third assumption is that how aid is given matters. For example, David Roodman (2004) and other members of the Center for Global Development have separately claimed that donors should give support for central government budgets (program aid) if governments are strong and benign, but should switch to support for particular projects (project aid) if governments are weak or corrupt. While this claim is plausible, Roodman does not support it with evidence. The World Bank's *Global Monitoring Report 2004* (2004) argues that aid is more effective in flexible forms like cash rather than as debt relief, emergency aid, or technical assistance. This claim too is plausible but unsupported. Other prominent figures—such as Ken Rogoff, former chief economist of the International Monetary Fund—have claimed that aid is more effective in the form of grants rather than loans. Once more, no evidence is given.

Since the claims about what makes aid effective are plausible but rest on modest evidence or none at all, we need a realistic view of what the quantitative indicators of aid quality actually show. These indicators are suggestive but hardly conclusive.

What indicators are out there?

The three main assumptions about what makes aid effective underlie several indicators of aid quality:

- *Poverty focus.* McGillivray (1989) constructed an income-weighted index running back to 1969. Aid to poorer countries receives a higher weight, with aid to a recipient with per capita income halfway between richest and poorest given a weight of 0.5. Roodman (2004), in a composite index, also gives a higher weight to aid going to poorer countries. Dollar and Levin (2004) measure the poverty "elasticity" of aid—how much aid flows vary depending on the poverty of the recipient country.

- *Policy or institutional selectivity.* Dollar and Levin (2004) also construct a policy elasticity measure, based on the Burnside-Dollar (2000) composite of good policy. Roodman (2004) weights aid depending on whether it goes to countries with good governance as measured by the popular Kaufmann, Kraay, and Zoido-Lobatón index (World Bank 2003). He adjusts the weights depending on whether the aid is project aid, said to be more appropriate for poorly governed countries, or program aid, thought to be suited to better-governed countries.

- *Restrictions and other measures of effectiveness.* Roodman (2004) penalizes technical assistance and aid that is tied. (Technical assistance must usually be purchased from the donor country, and tied aid must be spent on the donor country's products and services. Both typically reduce the purchasing power of the aid.) Roodman's attempts to make such adjustments are reasonable but ad hoc. For example, in a previous version of his annual paper he subtracted administrative costs, but he abandoned the idea in the 2004 edition after recognizing that high administrative costs might lead to better projects. Clearly, it is difficult to settle on a convincing measure of aid quality without better theories and evidence about what makes aid effective.

Which donors give high-quality aid?

Using several of these measures to rank the four largest donors and the two with the highest aid effort leads to one immediate conclusion: measures of aid quantity and aid quality seem to be correlated (table 1). The United States and Japan not only have the lowest effort among major donors (figure 1); they also do relatively little targeting of aid to poor countries and to those with good policy (as defined by Burnside and Dollar). This result is surprising, because there is no a priori reason to suspect that quantity, a focus on poverty, and a focus on good policy should be correlated. Indeed, Steven Radelet (2003) makes the logical point that efforts to increase the volume of aid will make it harder to be selective. There are several explanations for the apparent correlation. One is that it is easy to argue for more aid when the aid itself seems to be well aimed. Another is that when countries are committed to development, they perform well in several ways.

Still, the indexes sometimes agree less than might be expected—a warning to avoid reading a glib, intuitive message into an indicator that depends greatly on the technical details.

Table 1 | Ranking donors on aid effort and quality

Donor country	Aid effort[a]	Aid quality indexes		
		Poverty elasticity (Dollar and Levin 2004)	Policy elasticity (Dollar and Levin 2004)	Composite (Roodman 2004)
Denmark	1	1	1	3
United Kingdom	3	3	2	1
Norway	2	2	3	5
France	4	5	6	2
United States	6	4	5	4
Japan	5	6	4	6

Note: Rankings are based on 2002 data.
a. Aid effort is measured by official development assistance (ODA) as a percentage of the donor country's gross national income (GNI). The data are from World Bank (2004).

Figure 1 | The big donors, and the generous ones

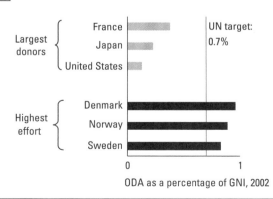

Source: World Bank 2004.

Are donors more focused on poor countries?

There is no sign that aid is becoming more focused on poor countries. McGillivray's income-weighted index shows very slight improvements in 1969–84 for the largest EU economies (the EU-4: Germany, France, the United Kingdom, and Italy) and for the multilateral agencies, but an overall fall in the poverty focus of the United States and no clear trend for Japan (figure 2). Dollar and Levin find that aid from all major donor groups became less responsive to poverty between the late 1980s and the late 1990s.

Are donors more selective?

For those who believe that aid works well in a good policy environment— now the consensus in the development community—there is more hope that donors are improving their aid targeting. Dollar and Levin find that the responsiveness of aid flows to good policy increased for most donor groups between the late 1980s and the late 1990s (see figure 2). The United States (from a low base) and Scandinavia (from a high base) showed particular improvements on this measure.

Roodman's composite aid quality index, which rewards donors for several important considerations—directing aid to poor countries and to well-governed ones, giving aid in an untied form, choosing appropriately between project and program finance—shows no clear trend in 1995–2002, however, except perhaps a convergence between the better donors and the worse ones.

Conclusion

Researchers are at last beginning to recognize that the quality of aid is as important as its quantity and to compute indexes accordingly. Those indexes suggest three observations:

- Relative to the 1980s, for any given income level of recipient, aid is increasingly aimed at countries with better policies.

- But aid is not aimed more at poor countries. Indeed, it seems to be targeted less to poor countries than in the 1980s.

Figure 2 **Little sign of greater poverty focus . . .**

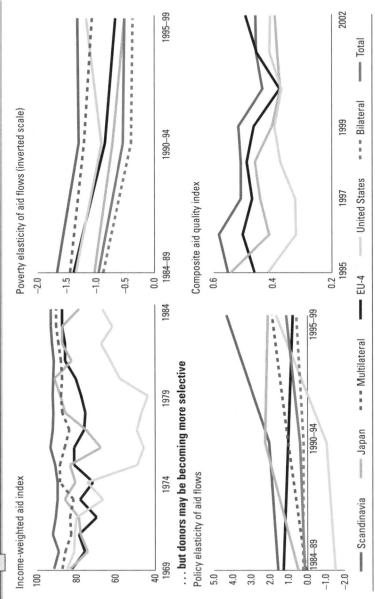

Note: The income-weighted aid index includes several measures of aid quality, including poverty focus. The composite aid quality index also includes several measures of aid quality, including targeting of well-governed countries.
Source: For income-weighted aid index, McGillivray 1989; for poverty and policy elasticity indexes, Dollar and Levin 2004; and for composite aid quality index, Roodman 2004.

- While a tradeoff might be expected between giving large quantities of aid and maintaining the quality of aid, the reverse seems to be true: the countries that give the most aid relative to their income also score well on different measures of aid quality.

Yet the caveats are as important as the conclusions, because the indexes are based either on narrow empirical research or on no research at all. One consequence is that indexes that would intuitively be expected to show similar things produce very different messages.

The real value of this embryonic work on aid quality is to highlight the importance of the issue and the scale of our ignorance. Hopefully, future measures of aid quality and donor performance will be able to draw on rigorous measures of aid effectiveness.

6

Private Finance

Are Private Loans and Charitable Giving Replacing Aid?

Private financial flows to developing countries, such as debt, equity, remittances, and private charitable giving, have increased dramatically over the past 20 years. One commentator has even trumpeted "the privatization of foreign aid." Since private charitable giving remains small and developing country governments are borrowing more, not less, from official sources, this claim is misleading. But unprecedented sums are indeed flowing to the private sector in developing countries.

Private financial flows are having a huge development impact in the countries receiving them, and the momentum seems to be picking up. Gross unofficial flows—foreign direct investment, migrant workers' remittances, portfolio equity flows, grants from nongovernmental organizations (NGOs), and loans without a sovereign guarantee— increased sixfold between 1970 and 1985, and nearly tenfold between 1985 and 2002, to exceed US$380 billion (figure 1). Official flows— loans, grants, export credits, and publicly guaranteed debt—were less than half this level in 2002, at less than US$180 billion. As recently as 1985 official flows had been three times as large as private flows.

Net flows give an alternative picture, because large repayments or profit repatriations can make gross flows huge even while net flows are small or negative. Net flows to the private sector in developing countries display clear patterns. Net debt and portfolio equity flows are trivial compared with foreign direct investment and gross remittances; private flows go mostly to middle-income countries (figure 2).

Foreign direct investment flows go largely to lower-middle-income countries—notably China, with 30 percent of the developing world's population and 39 percent of these flows.

Remittances, though smaller, have already outpaced official development assistance and would even exceed foreign direct investment flows if the data excluded China. (For a skeptical discussion of the data, see OECD n.d.) Moreover, while foreign direct investment flows to developing countries are roughly proportional to the size of their economies—with lower-middle-income countries overrepresented— remittances to low-income countries are large relative to the size of their economies (figure 3).

Remittances also are important because they go directly to households, often for spending on essentials or investing in a new house or business. The total flow is much more stable than foreign aid or foreign investment (Ratha 2003), because the income and number of migrant workers change slowly. Even recent money laundering laws have not dampened remittances, as many feared they would.

Other private cross-border giving—from foundations, corporations, religious groups, and membership-based NGOs—is apparently substantial, yet far smaller than remittances and other sources of devel-

Figure 1 **Unofficial flows far outstrip official flows to developing countries**

Gross unofficial flows (US$ billions)

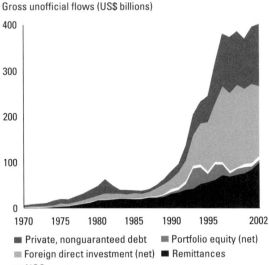

- Private, nonguaranteed debt
- Foreign direct investment (net)
- NGO grants
- Portfolio equity (net)
- Remittances

Gross official flows (US$ billions)

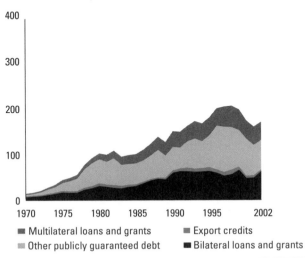

- Multilateral loans and grants
- Other publicly guaranteed debt
- Export credits
- Bilateral loans and grants

Source: World Bank, Global Development Finance database; OECD Development Assistance Committee.

Figure **2** **Direct investment and remittances top net private flows to developing countries**

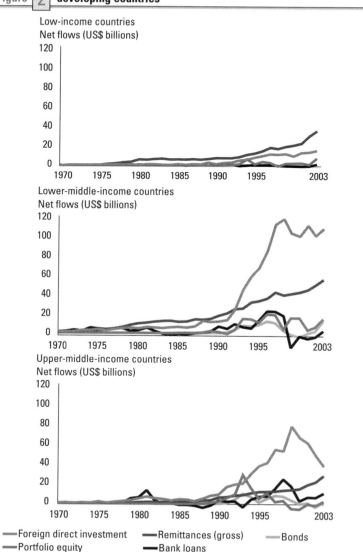

Source: World Bank, Global Development Finance database.

Figure 3 | **Where does the money go?**

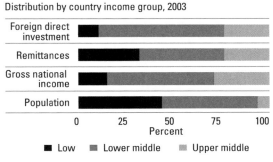

Distribution by country income group, 2003

Source: World Bank, Global Development Finance database.

opment finance. While this private charitable giving is poorly measured (box 1), figures on donations from the largest foundations (OECD 2003) suggest that annual private giving from rich countries is probably more than US$10 billion and less than US$25 billion. Compare these numbers with around US$70 billion of official development assistance and US$98 billion of remittances in 2002.

Changing patterns of commercial finance

What trends have emerged in investment flows—bonds, bank loans, and foreign direct investment? One way of interpreting the pattern of these resource flows to developing countries is as a shift from debt to equity finance (figure 4). This shift occurred in two stages: In the early 1980s net flows of debt collapsed because outflows rose sharply and (perhaps as a result) gross inflows fell. Then throughout the 1990s equity flows grew very quickly, mostly in the form of foreign direct investment.

Although net flows of private debt today are tiny compared with net foreign direct investment, gross flows of private debt remain quite large: US$247 billion in 2003, compared with net foreign direct investment of US$152 billion.

Box **1** **How well is private charitable giving measured?**

Data on private charitable giving reported to the Development Assistance Committee (DAC) of the Organisation for Economic Co-operation and Development (OECD) are patchy. For example, France, reported by DAC to be the fifth largest source of private giving in 1992, reports no data from 1996 on. Ireland's NGOs are implausibly reported to have given US$56 million, US$0, US$5.7 million, and US$90 million in a series of four years in the late 1990s.

Private giving also is vulnerable to double counting (Radelet 2005). NGOs receive funding from foundations and corporations and often substantial funding from governments too—all of which might be counted once when transferred to an NGO and again when disbursed by the NGO.

Recent estimates of U.S. private giving show big disparities. Adelman (2003) puts U.S. private giving at US$17 billion annually, arguing that the OECD figure of around US$6 billion underestimates the amount because most private donations are not reported. While Adelman has been criticized for lack of documentation, her estimate seems likely to be more accurate than the OECD figure.

Figure **4** **The shift from debt to equity**

Net flows to developing countries (percentage of total)

Source: World Bank, Global Development Finance database.

These gross disbursements of debt have undergone big shifts in composition over the past two decades. In the mid-1980s most debt flows from banks and bond markets to developing countries were publicly guaranteed. Now governments prefer to borrow from multilateral agencies (see chapter 3). Meanwhile, commercial banks have found no shortage of customers in the private sector (figure 5).

What explains trends in private finance?

So the major developments in private for-profit finance are a shift from debt to equity and a shift away from private debt with a sovereign guarantee. What might explain these trends?

As chapter 3 argues, the shift in sovereign borrowing from private sources to multilaterals seems to reflect responsible debt management: developing countries are seeking longer maturities and paying off debt. This implies that the decline in private, publicly guaranteed debt is a demand-side phenomenon. Private banks and bond markets could supply debt with long maturities but presumably feel it is too risky to do so, especially at interest rates that could compete with those of official sources.

Yet the demand for nonguaranteed private debt remains strong. The most likely explanation is the growing importance of the private sector in developing countries after the privatization and deregulation of the 1980s and 1990s.

Still, equity finance, usually in the form of foreign direct investment, is much more popular than private debt finance. One important reason is that equity finance shares risks in a way more likely to align the incentives of investor and recipient. Equity finance gives investors an upside risk and so encourages them to transfer technology and expertise. Direct investment also is less footloose than portfolio capital or short-term debt and thus attractive to recipient countries.

Moreover, the risk of expropriation for foreign direct investment is arguably lower than the risk of repudiation for long-term debt. This calculation depends on the investment climate and must be set against currency risk, which affects foreign direct investment but not dollar-denominated debt. This tradeoff has presumably swung in the direc-

Figure 5 **The rise of nonsovereign debt**

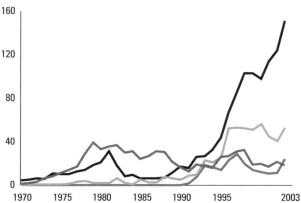

Gross disbursements (US$ billions)

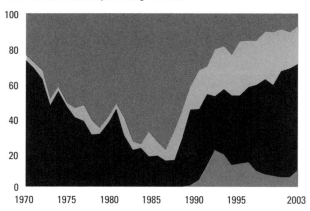

Gross disbursements (percentage of total)

Privately raised, publicly guaranteed debt   Private debt without public guarantee

◼ Commercial bank loans   ◼ Commercial bank and other loans
▦ Bonds   ▦ Bonds

Source: World Bank, Global Development Finance database.

tion of direct investment as typical (median) inflation rates have fallen in developing countries. As long as the investment climate in developing countries continues to improve, large flows of direct investment can be expected to persist.

Conclusion

Private finance is now the biggest show in town. But to speak of a privatization of foreign aid, as a provocative *Foreign Affairs* article (Adelman 2003) recently did, is going too far: developing country governments continue to borrow most of their debt from official sources, and private charitable giving is substantially smaller than official development assistance. But money from overseas is reaching the private sector in far greater amounts than a couple of decades ago, a large share of it remittances from migrant workers. Also very large are investment flows, which increasingly take the form of equity finance rather than debt finance, probably because direct investment has more attractive risk-sharing properties. And while much of this investment is bypassing the poorest countries, remittances are flowing in large quantities even there.

PART III

What Kind of Aid?

7

Aid and the Resource Curse

How Can Aid Be Designed to Preserve Institutions?

Many studies have found that countries with abundant natural resources grow more slowly than those without—a phenomenon often known as the "resource curse" or the "curse of oil." Some development specialists are concerned that foreign aid may also cause a resource curse. Recent research is not conclusive, but certainly does not rule out the possibility. This chapter suggests ways to avoid this risk and urges more attention be devoted to it.

Diamonds have not made Angola rich. Oil has not delivered prosperity to the República Bolivariana de Venezuela. Rich reserves of coltan (a mineral used in mobile phones) have fed war in the Democratic Republic of Congo. Indeed, countries with large primary export sectors (oil, rubber, diamonds, minerals) often, though not always, grow more slowly than their peers—a phenomenon recognized in mainstream economics as the "resource curse." Yet for many countries the key resource is not oil or minerals but foreign aid. Does foreign aid cause problems too? If so, why, and what can be done to prevent them?

How the resource curse works

Natural resource exports may damage economies in several ways (Harford 2003; Sala-i-Martin and Subramanian 2003). First, they create volatility in government revenues that, if poorly managed, will lead to inflation and boom-and-bust cycles in government spending. Second, they produce foreign currency earnings that, if not neutralized by monetary policy, will raise the real exchange rate, undermining the competitiveness of other sectors. Third, they can damage institutions (including governance and the legal system) indirectly—by removing incentives to reform, improve infrastructure, or even establish a well-functioning tax bureaucracy—as well as directly—by provoking a fight to control resource rents.

Although research is inconclusive, there is growing evidence that the third effect is the most problematic. (For reviews of the literature, see Sala-i-Martin and Subramanian 2003 or Djankov, Montalvo, and Reynal-Querol 2005.) There are both theoretical and empirical reasons to believe this. First, both volatility and exchange rate appreciation should be manageable with reasonable institutions and some political will. Second, "point source" natural resources like oil and diamonds—resources that are more easily controlled by an elite and do not need widespread labor, the rule of law, or infrastructure such as roads—have much more severe effects than other natural resources, such as agricultural products (Isham and others 2003). The implication is that it is not the volatility or the exchange rates that matter, but the fact that countries with point-source resources have weak institutions. Third, Sala-i-Martin and Subramanian (2003) show that natural resources appear to cause no direct drag on growth; the negative effects, while severe, are indirect and operate through the weakness of economic institutions.

Aid, oil, and institutions: new evidence

Might aid also damage institutions? Given the evidence on natural resource revenues, this possibility must be taken seriously. Several studies have shown that some aid money goes missing before reaching the intended recipients, and this money may well have properties similar to those of natural resource revenues, and for very similar reasons.

Knack (2000) reports evidence supporting this gloomy hypothesis. His econometric analysis shows that aid flows (relative to GDP and to government spending) are significantly correlated with a worsening of political risks for external investors, implying a deterioration in economic institutions (box 1).

Marshaling fresh evidence on the effect of both foreign aid and oil revenues, Djankov, Montalvo, and Reynal-Querol (2005) study changes in the quality of political rather than economic institutions. The results of their econometric analysis parallel those of Knack (2000): both aid and oil rents have a statistically significant and negative effect on democratic institutions.[1] On average, countries with above-average aid receipts relative to GDP promptly show a political deterioration. The effect of aid over the long run is substantial. A country receiving more foreign aid than three-quarters of the countries in the sample, over a period of five years, would expect to see a decline in the index of democracy by 0.6–1 point on a scale of 1–10.

Cases since the 1960s illustrate the effect (figure 1). The 10 biggest deteriorations in democratic institutions are associated with large aid inflows in the previous year, averaging 4 percent of GDP, well above the

---

1. The finding that oil damages democratic institutions replicates the results of earlier studies. While these studies often used oil exports relative to GDP as a measure of oil rents, Djankov, Montalvo, and Reynal-Querol (2005) use the dollar value of oil production (annual oil production multiplied by average oil prices for the year in question). This is a more direct measure of oil rents though it leaves aside production costs, known to be modest for most developing countries.

Box **1** **How to measure institutional damage?**

Although often closely correlated, the available indicators of institutional effectiveness measure different things.

Knack (2000) uses indexes from the International Country Risk Guide (ICRG), a commercial service providing subjective information on political risks facing overseas investors—in other words, the quality of economic institutions (http://www.prsgroup.com/icrg/ icrg.html).

Sala-i-Martin and Subramanian (2003) use an index produced by Daniel Kaufmann, Aart Kraay, and Massimo Mastruzzi on the basis of perception-based surveys of economic institutions such as the rule of law and the protection of property rights (http://www.worldbank.org/wbi/governance/govdata2002/).

Djankov, Montalvo, and Reynal-Querol (2005) use measures of political institutions: three indexes from the Polity IV database (http://www.cidcm.umd.edu/inscr/polity/) and the *checks and balances* measure from the Database of Political Institutions (http://www.worldbank.org/wbi/governance/pubs/wps2283.html). Two of the Polity IV indexes, *democracy* and *autocracy*, capture as objectively as possible political details: the competitiveness and the openness of executive recruitment, constraints on the chief executive, and the competitiveness of political participation. The third Polity IV index, *polity*, is simply *democracy* minus *autocracy*. *Checks and balances* reflects the number of veto players in a political system—the key decisionmakers whose agreement is needed before policies can be changed. Djankov, Montalvo, and Reynal-Querol produce similar results when they use the ICRG measures of economic institutions rather than their measures of political institutions.

mean. In contrast, countries with the 10 biggest improvements in democratic institutions received modest aid flows in the previous year, averaging around 1 percent of GDP. And the 15 episodes in which a country received one of the largest annual inflows of aid relative to GDP saw an average deterioration in the democracy index of 28 percentage points over the following year.

How aid might damage institutions and growth

Brautigam and Knack (2004) discuss several plausible explanations for the effects discovered in these econometric studies:

Figure 1   **Big inflows of aid are often followed by reversals in democracy**

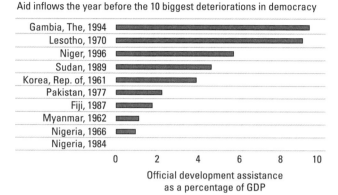

Aid inflows the year before the 10 biggest deteriorations in democracy

Gambia, The, 1994	
Lesotho, 1970	
Niger, 1996	
Sudan, 1989	
Korea, Rep. of, 1961	
Pakistan, 1977	
Fiji, 1987	
Myanmar, 1962	
Nigeria, 1966	
Nigeria, 1984	

Official development assistance
as a percentage of GDP

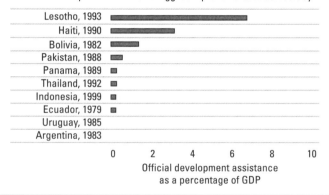

Aid inflows the year before the 10 biggest improvements in democracy

Lesotho, 1993	
Haiti, 1990	
Bolivia, 1982	
Pakistan, 1988	
Panama, 1989	
Thailand, 1992	
Indonesia, 1999	
Ecuador, 1979	
Uruguay, 1985	
Argentina, 1983	

Official development assistance
as a percentage of GDP

Source: Djankov, Montalvo, and Reynal-Querol 2005.

- *Aid can support poor governments and remove the pressure to reform.* The end of U.S. aid to the Republic of Korea and Taiwan (China) has been credited with their reforms in the 1960s. Large aid flows may eliminate the need to create a responsive, tax-collecting civil service, while a need to collect taxes enhances the capability and accountability of government. Aid-dependent governments are accountable to donors, not to their population.

- *The Samaritan's dilemma.* Aid creates a "moral hazard" problem, meaning that governments can spend money without a firm budget constraint, confident that donors will bail them out of any difficulty. Donors, who want to help (or are committed to send money for other reasons), may indeed be forced to oblige.

- *Aid siphons skilled workers away from government.* By paying big salary premiums, large donor projects can "poach" good people away from government, weakening its institutions.

- *Recipients overstretch themselves.* In a situation where focusing on priorities is important, recipients will often prefer to expand their operations to cover whatever projects donors wish to fund, especially since such funding often creates perks for officials.

- *Aid fuels patronage and sparks fights over rents.* Natural resources have provoked many wars—Iraq's invasion of Kuwait, the Biafran war in Nigeria, civil war in Angola, and the recent war in the Democratic Republic of Congo—but fights over aid are usually less obvious. Somalia's civil wars have been characterized as a fight for control of massive food aid, but most aid is not a physical resource that can be fought over and captured. Rent seeking presumably takes place at the level of political infighting, fraud, and theft.

Other explanations do not rely on an institutional effect. Rajan and Subramanian (2005) find that aid appears to slow the growth of labor-intensive industries in developing countries, consistent with a "Dutch disease" effect caused by an appreciating exchange rate. The World Bank (2000) finds that Africa's exchange rates seem to be overvalued—an effect that may be due to a combination of aid flows and natural resource earnings. Many aid specialists have also complained about the volatility of aid flows.

Using disciplines to preserve institutions

The results of the econometric studies should be treated with caution, especially since such cross-country statistical studies are fraught with difficulties. Nevertheless, at the very least these studies do not allow us to dismiss the concern about a "curse of aid." It is clearly a risk, and the first response should be to acknowledge that risk rather than treating institutions as if immune to the effects of aid flows. In the past few years, as development professionals have debated the proposition that "aid works in a good policy environment," donors have responded by redirecting aid to good performers. Too few have acknowledged the possibility that the aid flows may damage the policy environment. More knowledge is needed here, with case studies strengthening the preliminary cross-country research.

But beyond recognizing the problem and calling for more research, what practical steps suggest themselves? After all, just because aid may have caused problems in the past, especially during the cold war, does not mean that aid cannot be effectively delivered. (It is notable that large aid flows went in parallel with an improvement in the governance of many African countries during the 1990s, raising hope that methods of delivering aid have improved.) Aid does not have to cause the same type of damage as oil—but without appropriate disciplines, it might be just as bad. So what disciplines are available? There is some evidence that loans naturally discipline both borrowers and lenders more than grants do (see chapter 8)—but grants can be disciplined and loans lax. The key is to keep in mind the incentives facing both donors and recipients and design appropriate disciplines into aid packages:

- If the problem is that aid swells government budgets and thus discourages reform or the growth of accountable institutions, one solution is to direct aid away from governments. Direct budget support would presumably be particularly risky, but since most government funding is fungible, aid may be best delivered elsewhere. Using the private sector is clearly a possibility.

- If the problem is that aid generates rents and fuels patronage, the solution requires much closer control over the aid flows. Corruption needs to be vigorously fought. Donors and aid agencies can take a strong lead and can always look for ways to improve their efforts. One way is to eliminate discretion over rents by paying only after the desired results—vaccinations, electricity connections, operational rural phone booths—have been achieved. (For more on such output-based aid, see chapter 12 and also Brook and Smith 2001.)

The private sector can help here: one output-based model of disciplined aid uses the private sector to deliver results, providing grants only after those results are confirmed. This requires a combination of grants paid on completion, to cover the subsidy, and loans (from the private sector or from nonsovereign lenders such as the International Finance Corporation) to provide the capital necessary for the project. Some aid agencies have shown growing interest in such a combination—an interest that the research on aid and institutions should encourage.

Grants or Loans?

Development Finance and Incentive Effects

Some people think the best way to give aid is through grants. Others advocate aid embedded in subsidized loans. Mostly, incentive effects on donors and recipients are ignored in this debate. But grants and loans carry different incentives and in some settings can be complementary. Donors should offer a wider menu of options, including ongoing forgiveness of loans, unbundled subsidies, and loans combined with output-based grants. Donor agency staff should be rewarded for outcomes, not volume of funds out the door.

How is US$100 million of donor funding best delivered—through US$100 million of grants or through a larger volume of concessional loans with a "grant equivalence" of US$100 million? In a world of perfect capital markets there is no difference (box 1).

But capital markets are not perfect. That brings us to a hypothetical world that might be called the "development bank paradigm." In this world poor countries cannot tap private capital markets. But they do have a stock of good-quality development investments, the best of which also offer the highest returns. There are no incentive considerations: the money is always spent as promised, and always repaid. There is no uncertainty, and the donor agency can perfectly identify the best prospects.

In this world loans outperform grants. Both a grant and a loan of US$100 million would immediately be invested in a high-return project. The returns to the recipient from the loan would be reduced because the loan must be repaid, but the donor agency would immediately lend the repayments to the worthiest recipient awaiting a loan. By assumption, the relending of the money (reflows) has a higher rate of return than leaving it with the original recipient because the donor agency has a broader choice.

Box 1   How loans can be equivalent to grants

Assume a world of perfect capital markets, where all borrowers and lenders can borrow without limit at the same interest rate, 10 percent in real terms. If a country takes a concessional loan of US$100 million at 5 percent, repayable after one year, this creates a cash inflow of US$100 million this year and a cash outflow of US$105 million next year.

The country could convert the loan into a grant of about US$4.55 million by banking US$95.45 million and spending the rest. Next year the US$95.45 million will have earned enough at the 10 percent commercial rate to repay the US$105 million.

The country could also convert a grant into a loan. A grant of US$4.55 million can become a one-year concessional loan at a rate of 5 percent. The country simply borrows US$95.45 million commercially, for a total cash inflow of US$100 million. Next year the loan must be repaid with interest, a cash outflow of US$105 million.

Clearly, these assumptions are not realized in the real world. But in an approximate form they add up to the main justification for development banks lending to sovereign countries:

- Because there are good projects lacking capital, loans (subsidized or not) are useful.

- Because poor countries cannot tap private capital markets very well, development agencies provide those loans.

- Because the development banks believe that they can continually identify the most promising recipients, they ask for some repayment so they can relend the money.

Development finance in the real world

What's misleading about the development bank paradigm? The strongest advocates of grants typically take one or more of these positions:[1]

- Many projects will fail and even good projects do not generate high financial returns, so the loans won't be repaid without great hardship.

- Most countries are either capital constrained for good reasons or not badly capital constrained, so development bank loans do not correct any market failure.

- Reflows of aid money are neither large nor especially well allocated by development banks, so making a grant in the first place may be better.

In other words, critics of subsidized loans believe that grants are appropriate because the development bank paradigm is a bad description of the world. A more moderate view is that grants are sometimes

---

1. Ken Rogoff (2004) and the Meltzer report (IFIAC 2000) argue that development bank loans no longer correct a market failure. François Bourguignon and John Taylor, at a recent symposium, both drew attention to the fact that unsustainable debt is an argument against the use of loans (the transcript from the symposium, held October 1, 2004, at the Center for Global Development, is at http://www.cgdev.org/docs/grants%20and%20loans%20transcript.pdf). Taylor also argued for grants on the basis that social projects do not necessarily generate financial returns and that reflows are relatively trivial.

appropriate because the paradigm is not always a good description of the world—because capital constraints are not the problem or because past projects have failed, leaving an inability to pay off debt. A symposium reflecting a broad spectrum of views arrived at consensus on at least one point: grants are more appropriate in some circumstances, and loans in others.[2] This chapter aims to say more about those circumstances.

Incentive effects for recipients

Little can sensibly be said about grants and loans without considering incentive effects. For example, advocates of grants argue that debt-financed projects have not earned sufficient returns and countries therefore could not repay the loans. But the real problem was not loans but that the projects performed poorly. The burning question is whether grants or loans will be well spent in future. To answer it requires asking what incentives grants and loans produce for recipients and for donors. Let's start with the incentive effects for recipients.

Do grants reduce debt?

To argue that grants are appropriate for countries with severe debt problems seems sensible enough. The implicit assumption is that the grants will be used to pay down debt or for some legitimate development purpose. But is that true?

Clements and others (2004) show that an increase in grants tends to suppress domestic tax revenue. The effect is particularly stark for the most corrupt quartile of countries, in which 95 percent of grant money seems to be immediately dispersed as tax giveaways. By contrast, loans encourage revenue raising.

Odedokun (2004) finds a similar effect: grants reduce tax effort or encourage deficit finance. Moreover, grants, more than loans, promote government consumption spending and retard government invest-ment spending. Djankov, Montalvo, and Reynal-Querol (2004) also find that grants tend to raise government consumption, and loans to raise investment.

---

2. For details on the symposium, see note 1.

But Odedokun also finds problems with subsidized loans: recipient countries will demand an excessive supply of them. Unless subsidized loans are carefully rationed—here the donors need the right incentives—they may also encourage indebtedness.

This research is not conclusive. But it does provide some empirical backing for the theoretical insight that the cheaper money is, the less efficiently it may be used. Still, there are good reasons to provide cheap money to the poor. The important thing is that spending is disciplined. The right kind of grants or loans might produce the right disciplines.

Do grants promote growth?

Recent work on aid effectiveness asks in which countries aid produces economic growth. Few papers have tackled the question of *what kind of aid* produces growth. One that does is Sawada, Kohama, and Kono (2004). Decomposing aid flows into grants and concessional loans, the authors find that aid on average has no effect on growth (regardless of recipient policies), nor do grants. But loans to a country with good policies are associated with faster growth. Djankov, Montalvo, and Reynal-Querol (2004) find similar results: loans can promote growth in a good institutional environment, but grants do not.

That does not mean that grants are ineffective. Grants may support projects, such as providing primary school textbooks, that are not aimed at boosting medium-term growth. But more evaluation of this question would be valuable. Given Odedokun's finding that grants are spent on consumption rather than investment, the failure of grants to produce growth seems a cause for concern.

Incentive effects for donors

The incentives of donors are even less well explored than those of recipients. There are several issues of concern. First, that donors will provide less money (in gross terms) if they supply grants rather than loans. Second, that development banks that rely on loans have an incentive to push them even when inappropriate. And third, that aid agencies may be less assiduous in monitoring grants than loans, since they have no direct financial interest in the success of a project once a grant is made. Little evidence seems to exist on any of these questions.

Do grants reduce the volume of aid?

Since grants are more generous than loans, increasing the share of grants will necessarily reduce gross disbursements if donors refuse to increase funding levels. (Some aid agencies also fear that switching from loans to grants will place them at the mercy of unpredictable appropriation processes in donor governments.) Will they? Only up to a point.

Odedokun (2004), looking at official flows from 22 donor countries in 1970–99, finds that the larger the share of grants a donor makes, the lower the gross disbursements. The choice is indeed between a large volume of loans and a smaller volume of grants. But Odedokun finds no evidence that reflows are being used to fund current grants or loans: large shares of loans several years previously are not correlated with high disbursements today.

Do loans encourage "loan pushing"?

Critics of loans argue that development banks have a strong incentive to lend even when such lending is inappropriate. Reasons cited include a culture that values gross flows, and "defensive lending," in which official lenders provide loans to enable borrowers to repay existing debt.

Birdsall, Claessens, and Diwan (2003) found evidence of substantial defensive lending: donors to African countries in 1978–98 lent more to those with bad policies if they also had large existing debt.

Yet agencies given grants to disburse also face pressure to spend money, sometimes so quickly that it is impossible to find the best projects. The problem seems to be not whether funds are disbursed as loans or grants but what kind of behavior is rewarded. Both "loan pushing" and "grant pushing" need to be discouraged with appropriate incentives. A good place to start would be for donors to insist on accountability for development results rather than volumes disbursed.

Smarter development finance

The debate over grants and loans has been useful but too polarized. There are plausible objections to the use of grants:

- Grants increase government consumption and reduce investment spending.

- In corrupt governments grants are used to finance tax reductions.

- Grants do not seem to promote growth.

But the objections to loans are also powerful:

- Even heavily indebted countries are happy to secure subsidized loans, thus getting deeper into debt.

- Compounding this problem, development banks may push loans when they are inappropriate.

- Reflows from loans do not necessarily finance further aid.

These objections are really protests against sloppy development finance. Both grants and loans should be better monitored and evaluated. Development agency staff should be rewarded for producing good outcomes, not for handing out cash. And donors should explore more sophisticated approaches to development finance. Several proposals exist:

- *Ongoing forgiveness.* Loans could be made with predetermined conditions, to be independently audited. Every year in which the conditions are met, that year's loan payment would be forgiven. The loan would thus be converted into a grant, gradually and according to transparent conditions. (Alternatively repayment could be deferred until a predetermined condition is met, such as high commodity prices or high GDP growth.)

- *Unbundled subsidies.* A US$150 million subsidized loan can be regarded as, say, a US$50 million grant and a US$100 million market-rate loan. The funds could instead be offered as a US$50 million grant with an option to borrow up to US$100 million at market rates. That would leave the recipient free to take the loan only if appropriate; it would have no need to borrow to get the subsidy.

- *Loans combined with output-based grants.* Output-based grant schemes pay grants only on delivery of the desired output. But finance is also needed. The ideal is private finance, but output-based schemes, being generally experimental, may be slow to attract such finance. And loans with a sovereign guarantee undermine the disciplines behind output-based aid. That leaves development banks that lend to the private sector, such as the International Finance Corporation. Output-based aid is an attractive piece of financial engineering: the promise of the grant shifts purchasing power to the poor, performance risk is shifted to the private investor, and political risk is transparently priced because attracting investors to risky projects will be expensive.

Providing a menu of financing options is likely to produce better results than offering each borrower a particular type of aid, even if supposedly tailored to the borrower's needs. Lending without a sovereign guarantee should be part of this menu; it may help to address (but will not eliminate) the "moral hazard" problems of lending to countries that expect eventual debt forgiveness.

Better evaluation of the incentive effects of both loans and grants is urgently needed. The results should help design more effective aid, no matter how that aid is financed.

Aid Effectiveness

Can Aid Agencies Be Smarter than the Invisible Hand?

Private financial flows such as foreign direct investment seem to encourage economic growth and relieve poverty in part because they create excellent incentives for transferring know-how and in part because they are subject to a stern market test that ensures they are allocated and monitored carefully. For aid flows, not automatically subject to these disciplines, it is difficult to be as effective—but aid is needed because private flows bypass many of the poorest parts of the world. This chapter argues that aid agencies can learn what makes private flows so effective and use these lessons to bring better aid to the poorest.

Economic development requires money. Not only money, of course, but money matters—which is why the debate about aid often revolves around such issues as forgiving debt or giving more funding. Yet aid is no longer the major source of money flowing into developing countries, which now enjoy inward foreign direct investment, remittances from migrant workers, loans from banks and the bond markets, and substantial grants from nongovernmental organizations (see chapter 6).

These rival sources of money are certainly not perfect substitutes for aid. They flow to different countries and to different people within countries, on different cycles, bundled with different ideas and with different aims—and, not surprisingly, have different results. What do they teach us about aid?

Private finance and growth

First consider results. Djankov, Montalvo, and Reynal-Querol (2004), in a study of both private and official flows to developing countries, assess the indirect impact on economic growth, through government spending, as well as the direct impact, of private-to-private flows (loans and equity flows to the private sector), private-to-public flows (government borrowing from the private sector), and remittances—and the results look encouraging. The private flows do not raise government consumption (which is good, since high government consumption dampens growth), but they seem to increase total investment, which accelerates growth. A large body of research already shows that private-to-private flows directly boost growth.

This is not surprising. Ever since Adam Smith conjured the image of the "invisible hand," the ability of private enterprise to generate wealth for all has been widely appreciated. So should we abandon official aid and rely on private finance? Of course not, for several reasons:

· Private finance flows only to where money is to be made (see chapter 6). That inflows of portfolio equity increase economic growth or that foreign direct investment can be a superb way to transfer technology is no comfort to the victim of a tsunami or a civil war.

- The technology transferred by private finance is focused only on increasing the productivity of particular supply chains. Private investors have little interest in building rural roads or helping to design a legal system.

- Even if private finance produced superb development results, we would always hope to do more.

Why does aid fall short?

But matching the benchmarks carved by the invisible hand of private finance is difficult for official aid. One problem is that aid flows may weaken governance in developing countries, for example, by triggering a political struggle to control the cash (see chapter 7).

A second problem is that official aid does not seem to boost economic growth, at least not as irrefutably as private finance does. Djankov, Montalvo, and Reynal-Querol (2004) find that official development assistance as a whole directly reduces economic growth and also indirectly retards growth by increasing government consumption and reducing total investment as a share of GDP. This finding is broadly consistent with recent research on aid effectiveness, which fails to find a strong positive effect of aid on economic growth. Djankov and his coauthors also find that when a recipient's aid is mostly in the form of grants, the negative effects on growth are more severe.

These findings come from cross-country regressions, always treacherous. One possible complication is that bilateral agencies in the past tended to hand out mostly grants, while multilateral agencies typically used loans—so the apparent superiority of loans may result in part because multilaterals give more effective aid, whether grants or loans. Moreover, what was true in the past, especially during the cold war, may not be true in the future. And of course economic growth is not the only measure of development results, nor the aim of all development assistance. Nevertheless, the results are intriguing and consistent with earlier findings by Odedokun (2003) and Sawada, Kohama, and Kono (2004) (see chapter 8).

Why does aid seem to be falling short of its potential? The answer may be macroeconomic. For example, foreign aid may damage the competitiveness of the industries that developing countries would most expect to fuel growth. Rajan and Subramanian (2005) provide innovative evidence for this explanation.

An alternative explanation is that the failure of aid to promote growth is a statistical illusion: private for-profit flows will tend to seek successful, growing economies, while aid flows will tend to seek struggling ones. The apparent superiority of private flows may indicate that the statistical analysis has not fully controlled for this effect.

Benevolent, monitored, and "smart"

A possibility equally worth considering is that some private flows outperform aid because they generate the right incentives for those sending and receiving the money, incentives that are key to producing development results. At the risk of some simplification, it could be speculated that the development results of financial flows into developing countries depend on three qualities (table 1):

- *How benevolent is the finance?* The most benevolent finance flows to the poorest people in the poorest countries exactly when they need it and never needs to be repaid.

- *How well is the finance monitored?* Perfectly monitored financial flows go exactly where their owners want them to go. Imperfectly monitored flows might be spent on pet projects, stolen, or wasted.

- *How much knowledge flows with the finance?* Knowledge matters, whether provided as stand-alone advice or alongside financial flows. Much official aid is bundled with technical advice, but some private flows like foreign direct investment also come with advice and training.

The ideal development assistance would be benevolent, monitored, and "smart" in the sense of providing valuable know-how, but finance that falls short of this ideal can still be hugely useful. For example, the bond markets provide developing countries with finance that is indifferent to development results and contains no advice but without which the borrowers would surely be poorer. Workers' remittances are

Table ☐ 1   **Which financial flows have the key qualities?**

Qualities	Example
Benevolent, monitored, smart	Ideal development assistance
Indifferent, monitored, smart	Foreign direct investment
Benevolent, unmonitored, smart	Careless development assistance
Benevolent, monitored, dumb	Workers' remittances
Indifferent, monitored, dumb	Bond market finance
Benevolent, unmonitored, dumb	Populist emergency aid

"dumb" too, but since they are well meaning and well aimed, small wonder that development professionals are beginning to be excited by their potential to relieve poverty. Foreign direct investment is entirely indifferent to the development results it may cause—but those results often materialize where the investment is packaged with cutting-edge technological know-how. The question is, how to provide aid agencies and recipients with the same incentives to teach, learn, and achieve results as are automatically created by the "invisible hand"?

Can aid flows be monitored as well as private flows?

It could be argued—though it's hard to prove—that many private flows are monitored better than official aid flows. In some cases the monitoring is inherent: a migrant's remittances to his family back home can be closely monitored because the personal relationship is so close. (And some Mexican migrants open store credit accounts for their relatives rather than sending cash, so they can check that the money is spent prudently.)

But most financial flows are flows of other people's money. Aid agencies spend taxpayers' money. Private banks lend depositors' money. Multinational companies invest shareholders' money. Inevitably, such money will be assigned with less care than the personal income of those who manage these flows—the bureaucrats, bankers, or managers.

What stops complete chaos? Competition and good governance.

Is an organization like the World Bank or United Nations Development Programme governed less well than a publicly listed private company? Evidently not, if the company is Enron or Parmalat. Yet companies will always have a governance edge over governmental organizations: investors and depositors have a wide choice on where to put their money, which sharpens the pressure to offer excellent corporate governance and increases the returns to analysts and rating agencies that review that governance. Given sufficient competitive pressure, the market should deliver good corporate governance: Enron went bankrupt; aid agencies never do. Since they are subject to neither intense competitive pressure nor scrutiny from analysts and rating agencies, maintaining the highest standards of corporate governance therefore requires all the more effort and goodwill.

Can aid flows be as smart as foreign direct investment?

The smartest finance, in the right circumstances, is foreign direct investment. Many studies confirm this. Consider the manufacturing of car seats. Sutton (2005) finds that multinational joint ventures in India can bring error rates down quickly: one new factory moved from 2,085 errors per million to 65 in just three years. Domestic firms in India, emulating the multinationals and using knowledge gained as their suppliers, can also make dramatic progress: one firm eliminated 99 percent of errors within five years of adopting cutting-edge techniques.

There is no mystery why foreign direct investment sometimes provides such tremendous expertise:

- The investing firm has strong incentives to improve the expertise of local workers, suppliers, regulators, and partners.

- Workers and suppliers have a lot to gain (high salaries, lucrative contracts), and multinational auto manufacturers are careful to monitor closely and reward excellence.

The largest alternative source of smart finance is development assistance coupled with technical assistance, largely advisory services and training. For example, a loan to fund construction of a new electricity grid and power stations would come with advice on the scale and design of the new grid and on the regulatory framework needed to make it run efficiently. The potential of smart, well-monitored, and benevolent development assistance is huge. But development assistance may not create the same incentives as foreign direct investment—for the recipients or the technical experts—to make the lessons stick.

The strongest incentives to learn arise if the flow of money will be cut off for those who fail to do so. This condition may apply for a supplier of a multinational corporation, but not typically for an aid recipient. Foreign direct investment is automatically subjected to a tough market test, but aid projects are not. If aid agencies want a tough test, they have to create it themselves using more rigorous evaluation (such as the randomized trials done by the pharmaceutical industry) or rigorous benchmarks of the quality of a country's governance (such as the World Bank's Country Policy and Institutional Assessment, or CPIA).

The strongest incentives to teach arise if repayment is impossible unless the technical assistance works (or if recipients pay directly for the advice). This condition may apply for aid agencies that make non-sovereign loans and equity investments or stand-alone consulting arrangements, but an aid agency making a sovereign-guaranteed loan knows that the likelihood of repayment has little to do with the success of the project.

Remedies

Aid agencies strive to provide aid that is carefully monitored and bundled with high-quality technical assistance, but more can always be done. Aid flows could be as well motivated and as tightly monitored as the remittances workers send back to their families—and could carry the expertise of foreign direct investment, the kind that can induce a hundredfold reduction in errors in just a few years in India. How could that happen?

Aid agencies should learn from the distinctive advantages of different private financial flows. Remittances seem to be well aimed and well timed. Radical proposals to give aid vouchers to the poor are usually dismissed as a joke—but these proposals aim at providing purchasing power and choice to those who need it most, when they need it, with a minimum of waste and misdirection. A proposal that achieved those aims would be no joke.

Foreign direct investment has even more to teach aid agencies. First, the standards of governance required to make such investments work are high and rising. Foreign investors are mercilessly unforgiving of poorly governed countries and partners. Aid agencies, if they wish to help the poorest, cannot be so choosy, but they can seek the highest standards of governance for themselves—which implies embracing growing competition in the industry (see chapter 2) and encouraging searching evaluations by disinterested rating agencies.

Second, foreign direct investment often creates projects dependent on rapid technology transfer. Everyone involved has a strong incentive to learn or to teach as appropriate, and a stern market test weeds out those who do not. Aid projects are not subject to any such test unless the agency decides to use rigorous evaluation. Sovereign loans for aid projects are typically repaid regardless of the quality of the technical assistance; nonsovereign loans and equity investments provide sharper incentives to ensure that appropriate lessons are learned.

Unfortunately, the most desperate situations, where we would want to help the poorest with grants and free advice, are also those where it is most difficult to maintain the appropriate disciplines and make aid effective. But one possibility is to give performance-based grants (see chapter 12).

In all cases aid agencies can raise their game by providing better information about how aid is being spent and embracing competitive pressures. High-quality evaluation of projects and of aid agencies, combined with the political will to deliver better aid, should in a competitive environment improve the governance of aid agencies and the quality of the aid they deliver. In a well-functioning market for aid, aid agencies can perform their roles even better than the invisible hand.

PART IV

The Role of the Private Sector

Corporate Responsibility

When Will Voluntary Reputation Building Improve Standards?

Activists are often unhappy with the laws governing business behavior and with their enforcement. One strategy they use to alter the behavior of corporations is to target not the laws but the corporations, hoping that they will change without being legally obliged to. Sometimes firms do, because they would rather incur the costs of behaving "better" today than the costs of being "shamed" later. But how does this reputational mechanism work? Will it achieve the right standards? Which companies will it affect? And are there good reasons to prefer it to alternative ways of setting standards?

Many people feel that stronger rules or better enforcement is needed on a range of social, economic, political, and environmental issues. As the economy becomes increasingly international, more attention is directed to international rules or rules in other countries. But since institutions for setting and enforcing rules remain much stronger at the national level, changing rules elsewhere is not easy. History suggests that change is often achieved by war or, occasionally, economic sanctions. A less troubling way is by treaty, creating cross-border judicial systems. This process can be painfully slow.

As the international economy has apparently outgrown national political institutions, "corporate social responsibility" has once again become a hot topic. Large companies have always faced demands to exceed their legal obligations, especially when those obligations are thought to be weak. Now that many activists argue that the most important weakness is international rather than domestic, these demands increasingly target multinational companies, their suppliers, and other international businesses.

Corporate social responsibility means different things to different people. But for the purposes here, it is defined as socially minded behavior such as respecting human rights, refusing to pay bribes, caring for local communities, and adhering to environmental standards. A natural question arises: When is this corporate social responsibility a good substitute for other, more formal institutions, and when is it likely to disappoint? In other words, what is corporate social responsibility good for?

A reputational issue

Firms have several reasons to behave in socially responsible ways. One is simply that a corporate culture may value more than mere profit. A second is that social or environmental action can directly increase profit. Improving energy efficiency, for example, can reduce costs.

A third reason is that much corporate social responsibility is essentially a reputational game in which companies behave better in return for a better deal from customers, suppliers, employees, investors, or other stakeholders (Oxford Analytica 2000). For example, "socially responsible investing" is now big business, driven largely by screening strategies in which it is permissible to hold shares only in companies that satisfy such criteria as decent treatment of staff or protection of shareholder rights. Though held up as ethical, such behavior is often just sound business practice. Mainstream investors increasingly view socially responsible investment as good strategy. The idea, yet to be thoroughly tested, is that firms that behave well will find it easier to raise funds.

The most direct and well-known reputational effects result from campaigns against corporations accused of causing environmental damage or violating the rights of workers or indigenous people, such as the high-profile campaigns against BP, Nike, and Shell. These campaigns aim to achieve change by punishing the company. They may persuade stakeholders to boycott the company, leading to higher costs or lower revenue. And they may make it more difficult for the company to obtain licenses and approvals later on.

This is essentially a classic reputational mechanism. Stakeholders in a company expect it to adhere to certain rules. When it does not, the stakeholders "punish" the company by making its business less profitable or even putting the company out of business. That gives the company an incentive to conform to the stakeholders' expectations. Companies are also commonly rewarded for good behavior (such as "fair trade") through analytically equivalent mechanisms.

It would be wrong to presume that because corporate responsibility campaigns appear to be well intentioned they will have good effects. What is important is to understand the power of the reputational mechanism to achieve change and the social usefulness of the change achieved. Its power to achieve change is determined by the ease with which stakeholders can monitor compliance and punish cheating. Its social usefulness depends on the quality of the standards enforced.

When can reputational campaigns achieve change?

The reputational mechanism works when firms would rather incur the costs of behaving well today than pay the costs of being punished for misbehavior later. Game theory, more usually applied to understanding how cartels stick together, sheds light on when this will happen:

- Firms must be long-lasting and patient; otherwise the temptation to make a quick buck through dubious practices may prove overwhelming.

- Boycotts must be easy to inflict. Consumer boycotts in commodity markets such as gasoline require little effort by individuals. By contrast, employee resignations are costly to inflict and tend to have a significant effect only in the long term or when the stakes are very high.

- Offenders must be easily identified and monitored, so that firms know that if they step out of line, they are likely to be caught. Modern communications ease detection and monitoring (but also support false allegations).

- The costs of obeying the rules must be moderate compared with the costs of the reputational damage that can be inflicted.

The pattern of corporate responsibility campaigns is understandable in the light of this analysis. Campaigns have focused on large multinationals not because their ethical records are necessarily worse but because they are easily identified and in for the long haul. Campaigns have been most successful when targeting companies that sell into competitive consumer markets: consumer products are visible and easy to target, and competition makes it inexpensive for consumers to inflict boycotts. Producers of intermediate goods and services find it easier to evade boycotts.

Campaigns commonly target the market leader rather than the most irresponsible company, in the hope of achieving widespread change. This approach makes little connection between behavior and punishment and fails to create the right incentives for change. Sympathetic commentators have noted that corporate responsibility campaigns would have more effect if they gave companies more credit for doing things right (Freeman and Elliott 2003). Moreover, campaigns allow less prominent firms to escape censure, and these firms have refused to change their behavior.[1]

---

1. For example, Nike has put resources into setting up collaborative bodies for responsible behavior (Global Alliance, Fair Labor Association), but only a few competitors have joined.

Where campaigns demand improved behavior in general, rather than adherence to a particular (rigid) standard, companies can respond with relatively low-cost approaches. For example, Shell responded to pressure from environmentalists by beginning to publish detailed environmental and social accounts, supporting the Kyoto Protocol, and making a commitment to phase out gas flaring. Each of these actions has a relatively modest cost, measured in millions against annual profits of billions. Eliminating gas flaring can even create a profit stream.

By contrast, Shell refused to close its businesses in Nigeria despite a storm of protest after the execution of the activist Ken Saro-Wiwa and others by the dictatorship of General Sani Abacha. Leaving Nigeria would have cost the company billions of dollars, a cost far greater than any boycott could inflict.

Boycotts can rarely discourage every company. Large companies based in rich countries have more valuable reputations to protect than smaller companies and those based in developing countries. When Talisman Energy, a medium-size Canadian oil and gas company, quit its operations in Sudan, it did so not just because of activism but because of the risk that the United States would impose sanctions preventing it from raising capital on U.S. markets. Talisman sold its stake to India's national oil company, the Oil and Natural Gas Corporation, which clearly felt that neither activists nor sanctions could cause it enough damage to make the deal unattractive.

What are the right standards?

Economic interests and ethical values vary greatly, so it is hardly surprising that global standards for corporate responsibility are controversial. Any system of rules, whether voluntarily adopted by companies or negotiated in a treaty, would struggle to resolve such differences. Still, most parties in the corporate social responsibility debate could probably agree that standards should both pass a cost-benefit test (with costs and benefits broadly defined to include social and environmental issues) and favor the poor, not the rich. How might voluntary standards stack up against compulsory standards on these criteria?

On costs, voluntary standards might be expected to do well, since firms have a strong incentive to work out ways to satisfy their critics that are not prohibitively expensive. By contrast, compulsory standards, lacking the same flexibility, can impose high costs. One caveat: the cost of monitoring or reporting may be higher in an ad hoc voluntary system.

On the benefits side, there is less reason to be confident. The corporate social responsibility agenda naturally responds to high-profile, emotive issues, which do not overlap perfectly with areas where the most good can be done (Freeman and Elliott 2003). All parties in the debate have a responsibility to look for issues that offer the biggest benefits rather than those that are the most sensational. Multilateral agencies could provide valuable leadership by highlighting important but underexposed problems.

On the distribution of benefits between rich and poor, there is no doubt that the globalization of media reporting has made the corporate social responsibility agenda more global and more responsive to the world's poorest. Even so, a risk remains that companies will comply with standards by shifting costs to others—for example, by avoiding low-wage economies because of pressure about labor standards. That response may impose a small cost on the company but a big cost on the poor.

The risk of such unintended consequences is higher if campaigns for better standards depend on a superficial understanding by consumers— and if those affected by the new rules are excluded from the debate. On such issues as fair trade, climate change, and labor rights the global corporate social responsibility agenda may not always match local interests (Ward 2004).

The messy process of reputation-based corporate social responsibility campaigns may have an unexpected benefit: the process seems difficult for industry cartels to subvert. Regulatory capture has long been a risk for any system of compulsory rules. Social and environmental rules are no exception. One observer alleges that private firms that audit corporate social and environmental performance "have occasionally acted like vested interests" in private forums for setting international standards—and argues that voluntary regulations are less vulnerable to capture (Gordon 2000, p. 9). That makes sense, because "capturing" voluntary regulations would require capturing public opinion, arguably more difficult than subverting a bureaucrat.

Voluntary standards are no substitute for a benevolent, well-informed regulator. But since no such regulator will appear on the global scene in the near future, the reputational process of developing voluntary standards for corporate responsibility will continue to play an important role.

Policy implications

Viewing corporate social responsibility as a reputational game suggests the following lessons:

- *Reputation building is a minor issue for some firms.* Firms that are small and short-lived, make intermediate products, or have little presence in industrial countries are likely to be immune to corporate responsibility campaigns. Improving their standards may therefore require different approaches.

- *Reputation-based standards risk excluding less visible groups.* Those affected by proposed standards must have a voice; otherwise the standards supported by the reputational mechanism will not be the standards demanded locally.

- *Voluntary action will minimize costs but is less likely to maximize benefits.* Multilateral agencies therefore have an important role in ensuring that the corporate social responsibility agenda focuses on maximizing benefits rather than newspaper column inches.

- *Reputation-based standards are probably less vulnerable to regulatory capture.* Agencies should avoid supporting or endorsing standards that represent a cartel between companies and established narrow pressure groups.

- *Voluntary standards will be experimental and flexible.* Formal regulation can struggle to cope with a wide variety of sectors and geographic locations (Ayres and Braithwaite 1992). So flexibility that allows standards to evolve and firms to try something new should be seen as useful, not threatening.

• *Voluntary standards can lead to better things.* Voluntary standards can help build the consensus, expertise, and goodwill that can lead to binding standards (Gordon 2000). So despite the flaws of reputation-based standards, there is reason to give them time to develop.

As the corporate social responsibility debate develops, multilateral agencies such as the Organisation for Economic Co-operation and Development, United Nations, and World Bank Group have a significant part to play. In most circumstances they have little or no ability to set and enforce global rules. Yet within the reputational arena they have much influence as conveners or in supporting (or refusing to support) corporate codes of conduct.

Anarchy and Invention

How Does Somalia's Private Sector Cope without Government?

Somalia has lacked a recognized government since 1991—an unusually long time. In extremely difficult conditions the private sector has demonstrated its much-vaunted capability to make do. To cope with the absence of the rule of law, private enterprises have been using foreign jurisdictions or institutions to help with some tasks, operating within networks of trust to strengthen property rights, and simplifying transactions until they require neither. Somalia's private sector experience suggests that it may be easier than is commonly thought for basic systems of finance and some infrastructure services to function where government is extremely weak or absent.

Somalia is the quintessential failed state. After the autocratic regime of Siad Barre fell in 1991, the country collapsed into civil war. Peace has been established in some regions, but Somalia has only a limited government in the Northwest and no recognized government in the South. In these circumstances the private sector has been surprisingly innovative. Competition thrives in markets where transactions are simple, such as retail and construction. In more complex sectors, such as telecommunications and electricity supply, the private solutions are flawed but impressive: coverage has expanded since the 1980s, and prices are attractive compared with those in other African countries.

Only when it comes to public goods or to private goods with strong spillover effects—roads, monetary stability, a legal system, primary education, a cross-border financial system—does the state seem to be sorely missed. But even here the private sector has developed creative approaches that partially substitute for effective government. As a result, Somalia boasts lower rates of extreme poverty and, in some cases, better infrastructure than richer countries in Africa (table 1).

Private firms make do

Somali entrepreneurs have used three methods to compensate for the lack of effective government regulation (table 2). First, "importing governance" by relying on foreign institutions—for example, for airline safety, currency stability, and company law. Second, using clans and other local networks of trust to help with contract enforcement, payment, and transmission of funds. Third, simplifying transactions until they can be carried out with help from neither the clan nor the international economy.

Telecommunications: networks link up

Many local companies have teamed up with international giants such as Sprint (U.S.) and Telenor (Norway), providing mobile phones and building new landlines. Vigorous competition has pushed prices well below typical levels in Africa, and Somalia now has 112,000 fixed lines and 50,000 mobile subscribers, up from 17,000 lines before 1991. Yet

Table 1 Comparing Somalia on development

Indicator	Somalia	West Africa[a]	Neighboring countries[b]
Per capita household income (US$), 2002	226	501	438
Gini index, 1997[c]	40	45	47
Population living on less than PPP$1 a day (percent), 1998[d]	43	50	52
Roads (kilometers per 1,000 people), 1997	3	3	3
Telephones (per 1,000 people), 2002	15	9	10
Population with access to safe water (percent), 2000	21	59	60
Adult illiteracy rate (percent), 2003	81	49	35

a. Benin, Burkina Faso, Burundi, Cameroon, Central African Republic, Chad, Democratic Republic of Congo, Republic of Congo, Côte d'Ivoire, Gabon, The Gambia, Ghana, Guinea, Guinea-Bissau, Liberia, Mali, Mauritania, Niger, Nigeria, Senegal, Sierra Leone, and Togo.
b. Djibouti, Ethiopia, and Kenya.
c. The Gini index ranges from 0 (perfect equality) to 100 (perfect inequality).
d. PPP dollars are U.S. dollars adjusted for purchasing power parity.
Source: World Bank, World Development Indicators database.

not all is well. Calling every phone subscriber in Hargeisa, in the Northwest, would require connections from four telephone firms. But firms in Mogadishu have now agreed on interconnection standards, and those in Hargeisa appear to be following suit. The negotiations were brokered by the Somali Telecom Association, set up with the help of the United Nations and International Telecommunication Union (ITU) and headquartered in Dubai (*Somaliland Times* 2004).

Electricity: simple solutions yield results

Entrepreneurs have worked around Somalia's lack of a functioning electricity grid, payment systems, and metering. They have divided cities into manageable quarters and provide electricity locally using secondhand generators bought in Dubai. They offer households a menu of choices (daytime, evening, or 24-hour service) and charge per lightbulb.

Table 2 | Private sector coping strategies in Somalia

Strategy and application	Example
Importing governance	
Telecommunications	Somali Telecom Association, set up with help of United Nations and ITU and headquartered in Dubai, supports interconnection.
Finance	*Hawala* system uses financial infrastructure outside Somalia for money transfers. *Hajj* traveler's checks written with Saudi banks.
Air safety	Planes operate out of foreign airports and are checked there. Planes and crews are leased from international suppliers.
Legal system	Companies are often registered offshore.
Monetary stability	Economy is de facto dollarized.
Using clan systems	
Savings and insurance	Rotating credit associations use clan links to convene and enforce.
Social insurance	By tradition, destitute families do not pay for water. Families and clans extend credit to others to pay for water during droughts.
Legal system	Clan elders arbitrate disputes. System is less effective in cross-clan disputes but still used.
Simplifying transactions	
Electricity and telecommunications	Entrepreneurs divide up cities into manageable chunks and use flat tariffs (such as per lightbulb) for electricity.
Finance	Quiz on clan relationships used in place of sophisticated security.

Water: access but not cheap or safe

Public water provision is limited to urban areas, but a private system extends to all parts of the country as entrepreneurs build cement catchments, drill private boreholes, or ship water from public systems in the cities. Prices naturally rise in times of drought. Traditionally, destitute families have not had to pay for water, while the slightly better-off borrow funds from relatives. Nevertheless, after several years of drought the United Nations estimates that many families in the Eastern Sanaag have debts of US$50–100 for water. Moreover, access to safe water is low even by African standards because neither regulators nor the market have been able to persuade merchants to purify their water.

Air travel: outsourcing safety

In 1989 the national carrier (partly owned by Alitalia) operated just one airplane and one international route (United States Institute for Peace 1998). Today the sector boasts about 15 firms, more than 60 air-craft, 6 international destinations, more domestic routes, and many more flights. But safety is a concern. Airports lack trained air traffic controllers, fire services, runway lights, and a sealed perimeter against stray animals, and checks on aircraft and crew are inadequate. The makeshift solution: international outsourcing. Somali carriers lease planes, often with crews from Eastern Europe (the largest, Daallo Airlines, leases a Boeing from the United Kingdom, to boost customer confidence). And they operate out of Djibouti, Dubai, and Nairobi, using the facilities there to check aircraft safety.

Private courts: quick but limited

A recent effort to endow Mogadishu with a functioning court collapsed when the court tried to levy taxes and take over the privately run port of El Ma'an. In any case Somalia lacks contract law, company law, the concept of limited liability, and other key pillars of commercial law. In some cases Somalis have used offshore registration of businesses to import legal concepts and services. More commonly, disputes are set-tled at the clan level, by traditional systems run by elders and with the clan collecting damages.

Such measures are free—and fast by international standards. In a case involving the oppression of minority shareholders in a large live-stock company, out-of-court talks were preferred, the company con-tinued to operate successfully, and the dispute was settled amicably. But clan-based systems deal poorly with disputes outside the clan. In a dispute involving the telecommunications company Aerolite, the interclan committee of elders awarded the plaintiff from a weaker clan an unfairly small settlement, and since it was not enforced, he received nothing.

Currency: perfect competition for dollars

Sharp inflation in 1994–96 and 2000–01 destroyed confidence in three local currencies. U.S. dollars are harder to forge, do not need to be carried around in large fragile bundles, and, most important, retain their value. The feeble capabilities of the central bank have allowed free entry into the currency exchange business, which is as close to perfectly competitive as is ever likely to be possible.

International fund transfers: *hawala* system

The *hawala* system, a trust-based money transfer system used in many Muslim countries, moves US$0.5–1 billion into Somalia every year. A person in New York wishing to send money to his family in Tog-waajale gives the *hawala* agent in New York the sum in cash, paying a 5 percent commission. The agent deposits the cash in a local bank account to be transferred to the company bank account in Djibouti or Dubai, then alerts the clearinghouse in Hargeisa, which passes details on to Tog-waajale. When the recipient shows up, the local agent quizzes him about his clan lineage using questions provided by the relative overseas as security against fraud. The transaction is usually completed within 24 hours. *Hawala* networks are unregulated and do not always keep records of transactions, but they are coming under pressure from efforts to combat money laundering (Omer 2003).

Savings accounts and traveler's checks

Somalia has adopted the widespread African institution of rotating credit associations, which rely on clan links for enforcement and provide a safe haven for savings. More innovative is the system of traveler's checks for the pilgrimage to Mecca, or *hajj*. Nobody would accept Somali checks, so Somali firms set up accounts in Saudi banks and write checks to pilgrims that can be cashed in any branch.

Gaps in private sector provision

In some areas the private sector has made little progress. The Somali road system, for example, is limited and in poor condition. For a private supplier to build a road and collect fees to cover the costs is apparently too hard, partly because of prohibitive transaction costs and partly because fee-paying users are not the only ones who benefit from roads.

Primary education is another disappointing story. Some 71 percent of primary schools are privately owned (typically by parents or communities), but enrollment is just 17 percent. By contrast, it is 82 percent in West Africa, where countries are richer and more stable and the government is much more heavily involved in the economy.

Ideally, benevolent government would sort out both problems. But government that is merely stronger might not help. Where municipal governments along the Berbera–Hargeisa road have the power to collect tolls, they do not spend them on maintenance. The failings of the education system are partly because half of Somalis are nomads. It is not clear that government would do much better, especially since the private schools are locally acknowledged to be superior to those run by local government. Rather than try to create a government system from scratch, a better policy would be to improve the network of higher-quality private schools.

Conclusion

The achievements of the Somali private sector form a surprisingly long list. Where the private sector has failed—the list is long here too—there is a clear role for government interventions. But most such interventions appear to be failing. Government schools are of lower quality than private schools. Subsidized power is being supplied not to the rural areas that need it but to urban areas, hurting a well-functioning private industry. Road tolls are not spent on roads. Judges seem more interested in grabbing power than in developing laws and courts.

A more productive role for government would be to build on the strengths of the private sector. Given Somali reliance on clan and reputation, any measures allowing these mechanisms to function more broadly would be welcome; credit and land registries would be a good start. And since Somali businesses rely heavily on institutions outside the economy, international and domestic policies supporting such connections would help.

For governments and aid agencies, the capability of some business sectors to cope under the most difficult conditions should give hope and guidance in other reconstruction efforts. It may take less encouragement than is commonly thought for stripped-down systems of finance, electricity, and telecommunications to grow.

Output-Based Aid in Cambodia

Private Operators and Local Communities Help Deliver Water to the Poor

By Yogita Mumssen

After decades of war and social disruption in Cambodia, publicly run water and sanitation services are scarce and limited mainly to urban areas. Most communities have had to rely on self-provisioning, and this has increasingly meant turning to unlicensed and unregulated private providers. But while private providers offer relatively good service, their high one-time connection charges put that service out of reach for all but the more affluent. Exploring how best to reach unserved areas and poor people, the government of Cambodia is piloting an output-based approach in four towns.

Cambodia is among the world's poorest countries, with per capita income of only US$321 a year and 41 percent of its population below the poverty line in 2002. Only a third of Cambodians have access to a safe water supply, and the record tends to be worse in rural and peri-urban areas. The result is one of the world's highest rates of infant mortality and morbidity caused by water-related diseases.

Publicly owned and operated water utilities provide service in Phnom Penh as well as more rudimentary service in several provincial towns. But because of decades of war and social disruption most communities have had to rely on self-provisioning. Many have made long-term arrangements with unregulated and often unlicensed private water vendors. While many of these vendors are small, some have invested thousands of dollars to deliver piped water service to customers.

Customers of the private utilities, some of which have recently been licensed by the government, are happier with the service received because its availability and quality are better than that provided by publicly run utilities. But much of the population cannot afford the service the private companies offer, because of the high tariffs and, even more important, because of the high one-time connection fees (Garn, Isham, and Kahkonen 2000). Moreover, the bidding processes for the contracts these companies won were not always transparent or competitive, and regulatory monitoring, if it exists at all, tends to be weak.

Testing the water with output-based aid

As part of an initiative to deliver water and sanitation services throughout Cambodia, the government is seeking ways to bring the benefits of privately run water services to unserved areas and especially to poor people. Using funds from an International Development Association (IDA) credit, it aims to provide water and sanitation facilities in about 23 towns through different forms of public-private partnership. Four of these towns will use an output-based aid (OBA) mechanism through design-build-and-operate contracts, while the other 19 will use design-build-and-lease (DBL) contracts. (The exact number of towns will depend on the government's final investment plans and on bidding results.) All the contracts will cover 15 years.

Designing the contracts

The four OBA contracts differ in design and implementation from the DBL contracts for one reason: to target connection subsidies to poor households. The provider will receive a subsidy payment for connecting each targeted poor household, while it will charge all other customers directly. Payment under the OBA contracts will be based on performance: the operator will receive most of its payment only after connecting poor households. But to reduce payment and prefinancing risk, the government will pay 5 percent of the total contract amount after the operator completes the initial drilling for deep wells and another 5 percent after it completes the detailed design and engineering of the system. The government will pay 80 percent of the subsidy per connection for all connections invoiced after receiving certification for each connection from an independent engineer. It will pay the last 10 percent (a "functional guarantee") after water quality and hydraulic testing are done for each system. Late payments will include a modest interest penalty.

Because the operator will be paid the amount it bid, regardless of how much providing each connection actually costs, it has an incentive to make the connections as efficiently as possible. While the contracts detail technical specifications to some extent, they allow enough flexibility so that the operator can use the most efficient and effective means of meeting the service standards and requirements. A new regulatory entity—the Contract Administration Unit in the Ministry of Industry, Mines, and Energy—has been created to verify that operators do not reduce the costs of connections by lowering standards. An independent engineer will perform the verifications initially, until the regulator develops sufficient capacity to do so itself.

In contrast with the OBA contracts, the DBL contracts are not performance based. Instead, the private operator is paid on the basis of inputs. The operator must provide a connection to anyone within its initial service area without charging a connection fee. The costs of connection are covered by the IDA credit. As a result, the implicit capital expenditure subsidy under the DBL contracts is both higher than in the OBA schemes and spread over all customers, rich and poor. So the OBA schemes may be a relatively efficient use of subsidies, depending on the costs associated with targeting.

The main implementing agency for the IDA-funded water supply projects is the Ministry of Industry, Mines, and Energy, which, along with its Contract Administration Unit, has overall responsibility for controlling quality, scheduling activities, and monitoring performance. As regulator, the Contract Administration Unit will ultimately verify the quality of service provided, though here again initial verification will be undertaken by an independent engineer. Connection prices and tariffs are detailed in the contracts, and tariff adjustments will be made as needed by the Contract Administration Unit. More detailed monitoring and regulatory arrangements are being developed alongside a more comprehensive regulatory framework.

Awarding the contracts

An open tender was held for the OBA contracts, with private service providers bidding on the basis of the lowest subsidy required to provide a connection to households in each of the four pilot towns. Of the eight firms preselected to bid, two made offers—a Cambodian company and a joint venture between a Cambodian and a Singaporean company. The joint venture, SINCAM, won all four OBA contracts (and eventually a few DBL contracts as well). SINCAM bid 22–28 percent less for the contracts than the public sector comparator price of $500 per connection—the total capital expenditure per household incurred by the government for similar donor-funded water projects in the past (figure 1). The OBA contracts were signed in March 2004.

The government believes that future OBA schemes will generate even more interest once greater efforts are made to disseminate information about such schemes and once their benefits for the poor and for the private operators become clearer. The presence of an international agency like the World Bank—through the IDA grant funding of the subsidies—to backstop the flow of payments to the private operator has helped reduce the risk and attract small and local players.

Community participation: targeting subsidies and building capacity

Two criteria were used to select the four OBA towns. First, the proximity of the town areas to one another, to provide possibilities for some

Figure 1 **Winning bids for the output-based aid contracts, by service area**

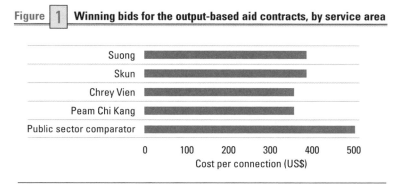

economies of scale and perhaps scope that could generate interest among private providers. And second, location along the route between Phnom Penh and Ho Chi Minh City, a dynamic area with relatively strong economic growth that could attract private operators because it includes not only low-income customers eligible for subsidies but also a large and growing population of middle- and high-income customers able to pay for service.[1]

After the pilot towns were selected, the next step was to determine which households would receive the connection subsidy. Communities played a big part in this. A household survey was developed within the communities to collect data, and village representatives and commune council members together determined poverty criteria. Based on these criteria and the results of the survey, the communities themselves identified the poor households that would receive the subsidy (table 1). An independent consultant later randomly verified the selection of households (O'Leary 2004). The survey also provided a way to inform households about the reforms being undertaken in the water and sanitation sector.

After the poor households were identified, a series of consultations were held in about 50 villages within the four pilot towns. These consultations provided another opportunity to inform households about the project. They also allowed an opportunity for introducing the con-

---

1. Compared with the OBA pilot towns, those chosen for DBL contracts generally have lower growth potential, which should mitigate the less pro-poor subsidy targeting implicit in those contracts.

Table 1 | **Households eligible for the connection subsidy, by service area**

Service area	Total households	Households eligible for subsidy[a]
Suong	4,408	990
Skun	2,578	1,004
Chrey Vien	2,682	354
Peam Chi Kang	3,456	660

a. These are the initial numbers of households determined eligible for the subsidy. In some cases the numbers have been revised slightly, usually upward.
Source: O'Leary 2004.

cept of water user groups to represent villages and towns—eventually called Clean Water Groups—and identifying likely candidates for the groups. These village consultations involved more than 1,600 household members, most of them women (O'Leary 2004).

Community consultations, including discussions relating to ability and willingness to pay, were also used to determine appropriate tariffs and connection fees for middle- and high-income households. And consultations about appropriate payment methods—such as installments or one-time payments—led to a decision to include different options in the service contract between the provider and each customer (O'Leary 2004).

Progress so far—and next steps

Although the OBA schemes are still at a very early stage, the Cambodian government has so far generally considered them a success. Implementation has gone well, perhaps because the communities made the main decisions about who receives the connection subsidy and were also consulted about fees and payment options. Participation has also been key in building capacity and disseminating information within communities—and all this has led to a broad sense of ownership in the outcome of the OBA schemes. The private operator has also made clear progress. SINCAM has identified and tested potential water sources and will soon undertake an environmental impact assessment. Construction is under way, and connections should be made in 2005.

While the OBA mechanism enables the poor to gain access to service through the connection subsidy, it does not tackle the problem of affordability of consumption, since all water users pay the same rate per cubic meter of water consumed. So far, tariffs for private network providers have been set so as to allow them to recover their costs. Whether any detailed formula is used in practice is unclear (O'Leary 2004). With tariffs for the OBA pilot towns ranging from 1,800 to 2,000 riels (around US$0.50) per cubic meter, households will spend an average of about 4.1–6.4 percent of their income on water (based on data from O'Leary 2002). Because these are average figures, poorer households—those eligible for connection subsidies—can be expected to spend a larger share of their income on water bills, perhaps even if (as is likely) they use other sources for some activities. A rough rule of thumb for the acceptable level of spending on water is around 5 percent of household income. Tariff-level affordability is an important issue being discussed by the Cambodian government, the World Bank, and the communities themselves.

As part of the initiative to increase private participation in water and sanitation, the World Bank and other donors are advising the government on the introduction of a new water act to strengthen the regulatory framework. A clearer, more transparent framework not only would help protect customers from abuse by private operators but also should provide operators with greater certainty.

The initial success of the project has prompted more such schemes in Cambodia, and a second batch of four towns is being prepared for a similar OBA mechanism. More than 1,660 poor households have been identified as eligible for a connection subsidy, and more are being considered, depending on available financing. Bidding for these towns should take place in 2005.

PART V

The Future of Aid

Scenario 1

The Rise of the Undergrowth

Imagine that you are in 2030, reviewing the aid industry over the past 25 years. This chapter offers one possible scenario— booming private remittances and nongovernmental aid flows put to innovative uses, eclipsing a less agile, more politically driven official aid industry. Chapter 14 offers a second scenario. Organizations use scenario planning to prepare for the very long term. Good scenarios are plausible stories about the future, recognizable in the trends of today. The ideal scenario encourages thinking about possible responses. It is in this spirit that this scenario is offered.

Trends to 2005

It was clear by 2005 that three trends were shaping the aid industry. First, incomes had been rising rapidly in many developing countries over the previous few decades, especially in East Asia and India. Fewer countries were very poor.

Second, more developing countries were able to borrow from banks or bond markets at attractive terms. And much of the money flowing to developing countries was no longer government debt but private borrowing, equity and foreign direct investment, and even remittances from migrant workers.

Third, new players—official agencies and unofficial ones, usually called nongovernmental organizations (NGOs)—had been entering the market for aid, a market that had seen a century of entry by aid agencies and no exit (see chapter 2). The new entrants were not only of the traditional type—from new donors such as China, Slovenia, and Thailand—but also of entirely new types—agencies with different approaches to raising or disbursing funds. These new types included the Millennium Challenge Corporation, distributing most of its grants to countries meeting objective standards, and the Global Fund to Fight AIDS, Tuberculosis, and Malaria, focusing on a tight group of cross-border problems.

2005–10: political aid returns

During the 1990s there was reason to believe that the quality of aid was improving. By most measures aid from major donors was aimed more at countries with sound policies, while aid from the world's largest donor, the United States, was focused more on poor countries in 2000 than 10 years earlier (see chapter 5).

Looking back from 2030, it is obvious that the 1990s were a brief "golden age" between the end of the cold war and the start of the so-called war on terror. In the early 21st century aid again became for most donor countries largely a tool of foreign policy—a legitimate tool perhaps, but it was always evident that the result would be aid that was not necessarily aimed at the poorest or the best reformers, and aid delivered without much interest in evaluating development impact.

The repoliticization of aid was widespread, noted by the World Bank as a clear trend in 2004. At the same time new players were rising: fast-growing China and India, reemergent, oil-rich Russia, and smaller countries such as Slovenia and Thailand were all taking steps to establish their own aid agencies and aid systems in the early years of the century. (In 2030 China's economy, with a per capita GDP of US$10,000, is clearly about to overtake the U.S. economy.)

The multilateral agencies were the most obvious victims of repoliticization: major donors withdrew support and resources in favor of their own programs. Why should donors fight political battles in the boardrooms of such institutions when they could retain complete control over their own aid programs? What interest did the United States have in supporting specialized United Nations agencies? Why should Brazil, China, or India borrow from institutions whose voting structures were stacked against them when private money was available just as cheaply? Regional and international financial institutions found themselves operating under tight conditions. Bilateral aid, less carefully targeted at the poor and less focused on sound policy and institutions (see chapter 5), grew in importance. Subcontracting and competition in the official aid industry withered, as governments wanted tight control of their aid programs and kept things in-house or relied on a few trusted contractors.

People power takes up the slack

But this shift was not a simple return to the politicization of the 1960s and 1970s, and competition and innovation were not dead. Big changes had occurred—in the attitude, resources, and awareness of ordinary people.

Many of these changes were already visible by 2005. For example, it was clear by then that remittances were going to be a critical competitor of official aid. They had been shown to be more stable (Ratha 2003) and a better prospect for boosting economic growth (Djankov, Montalvo, and Reynal-Querol 2004). These findings emphasized what should have been obvious: person-to-person transfers are likely to be well targeted and well spent. Between 1988 and 2001 remittances grew from less than half to more than twice official flows. Even in the poorest countries they exceeded official flows, and foreign direct investment as well.

Between 2000 and 2020, as the costs of wiring money home fell dramatically and international migration continued to increase, remittances grew even more important. A drop in average wiring costs from 13 percent to 3 percent between 2000 and 2010 saved US$10 billion annually—more than the disbursements of the International Development Association (IDA)—encouraging yet larger remittances (figure 1). Meanwhile the share of the world's people working outside the country of their birth more than doubled, from 3 percent to nearly 8 percent by 2020, sucked in by the demographic deficit in rich countries and accommodated by policies that created different categories of guest workers—and even allowed the issuance of driver's licenses for illegal immigrants, as seen in several U.S. states as early as 2003. By 2020 remittances had grown to nearly US$200 billion, dwarfing official aid flows.

Figure 1   Remittances: falling cost, growing volume

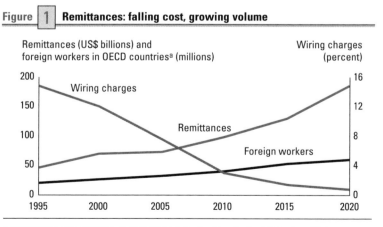

Remittances (US$ billions) and foreign workers in OECD countries[a] (millions)

Wiring charges (percent)

a. Excludes Canada, Germany, Greece, Iceland, Mexico, New Zealand, Poland, and Turkey because of data unavailability.
Source: Historical data from Ratha 2003 and OECD 2002; authors' projections.

More impersonal charity was also hugely important. Though still modest compared with official development assistance, annual grants from NGOs exceeded concessional loans from governments as early as 2002[1] and more than doubled to US\$20 billion by 2010. Charities were simply getting better at fund-raising, in an environment where there was plenty of money around. Oxfam's Christmas campaign in 2004 was one example: rather than giving Christmas presents, people flooded to the Oxfam Web site to buy chickens, school desks, even water tanks for an entire town (BBC Online 2004). Shortly afterward a huge public response to the Asian tsunami left governments scrambling to raise their own aid. In the United Kingdom private donations exceeded the government's initial package within 48 hours (Reynolds 2004). By 2010 massive giving campaigns, often coordinated by religious organizations, were making these earlier private efforts look small by comparison.

2010–20: the "undergrowth"

Altruism, in the form of both remittances and charitable donations, was important. Yet altruism did not motivate most private flows. Even before 2000 it was becoming clear that private for-profit lending was posing serious competition to loans from governments and development banks. This lending was just the precursor to a huge variety of new ways for finance to flow to poor countries and especially to poor people. By 2005 Mexican mortgage companies were operating in the United States, offering mortgages to emigrants to build homes back in Mexico—a business model that was commonplace by 2015.

Even more important than the raw volumes of private financial flows was the innovation they provoked. A new generation of mutual funds arose with the aim of directing investment to profitable local projects in developing countries. They were fueled by growing retirement savings in rich countries, hungry for returns, and by an awareness that the most

---

1. Data are from the Development Assistance Committee of the Organisation for Economic Co-operation and Development (OECD).

difficult operating environments presented the least competition. This trend was instrumental in raising standards of corporate governance (Klein and Harford 2004), increasing rewards to local expertise, and strengthening the business climate in poor countries.

Citizens of poor countries became far better connected, improving the effectiveness of aid, government spending, and private business. In 2004 a month of Internet use in Nigeria cost US$85, but Vietnam had already slashed costs to US$20.[2] By 2010 Internet service was available almost anywhere on the planet for a few cents a month. By 2020 two-thirds of the world's population had used a mobile phone. The easy access to information made it far simpler to tap into global best practices in health, agriculture, accounting, or food hygiene. Just as profoundly, it ensured that governments were held accountable. As early as 2001 the Ugandan school system had been transformed by the public dissemination of information about how much grant money each school was supposed to receive: the median amount received rose from nothing to more than 80 percent of the amount budgeted (World Bank 2004b).

Poverty was caught in a pincer between highly effective private giving and job-creating, growth-producing businesses. All these improvements spilled over into the burgeoning unofficial aid industry, which some term the "undergrowth." It gradually became clear that unofficial aid projects were delivering far higher returns than official ones. By 2020 that was provable beyond reasonable doubt. Internet platforms made it effortless for private donors to find worthy projects that were well governed, professionally managed, and fully certified. Independent monitoring and certification became a large and competitive business: charities and aid agencies were expected to demonstrate results, just as companies were expected to generate profits and produce audited accounts. Transparency and accountability became commonplace. In 2020 citizens of rich countries could order a new well or power generator for delivery in Sudan as easily and with the same assurance as they could order flowers for delivery to their grandmother in 2005.

---

2. Data are from the World Bank's World Development Indicators database.

The end of official aid?

Events of 2020–30 have left many commentators concluding that we have seen the end of the official aid industry. The few big infrastructure projects that cannot be handled by the private sector—such as in pariah closed economies—have been picked up by the Chinese and Indian development banks. Health, social, and environmental aid is now provided by such a vibrant, efficient, and well-funded combination of charity and private business that it is hard to see where the dinosaurs of official aid fit in. The only function left for them is knowledge management—consulting, research, and spreading best practices. Even this work is funded largely by universities, foundations, and user fees. Looking back, we can see that official aid once had an important role to play in development, but those times are long gone.

What does the "undergrowth" of the aid industry look like today? It defies description. We see a huge range of approaches, some experimental and some well established.

Consider a typical output-based aid project in Cameroon. It is designed by a small but expert Cameroonian service company, delivered by a huge Chinese multinational contractor, financed by a New York–based investment bank, and ultimately funded by donations gathered from all over Europe with the help of favorable tax treatment and an "aid matching" Web site. It seems quaint to suggest that government-to-government aid, long discredited in the eyes of rich and poor people alike, would have anything to do with such a project.

Economist Paul Seabright (2004, p. 15) reports that after the collapse of communism a senior Soviet official seeking advice on the workings of capitalism asked, "Who is in charge of the supply of bread to London?" An aid agency official transported in time from 1990 to 2030 might ask a similarly naive question about today's aid system. Nobody—not even a small group of institutions—is in charge of the aid industry of 2030.

Scenario 2

The Big Push

This chapter offers a second scenario, looking back from 2030 to review the aid industry over the past 25 years. The story is initially similar; then the scenario describes the response of the aid industry to falling numbers of people in poverty and to the growing ability of poor countries to borrow from the market. Well-meaning efforts to coordinate aid initiatives initially backfire. But they lay the foundation for a revolutionary system of managed competition between aid agencies and other players in the industry.

Trends to 2005

It was clear by 2005 that three trends were shaping the aid industry. First, incomes had been rising rapidly in many developing countries over the past few decades, especially in East Asia and India. Fewer countries were very poor.

Second, more developing countries were able to borrow from banks or bond markets at attractive terms. And much of the money flowing to developing countries was no longer government debt but private borrowing, equity and foreign direct investment, and even remittances from migrant workers.

Third, new players—official agencies and unofficial ones, usually called nongovernmental organizations (NGOs)—had been entering the market for aid, a market that had seen a century of entry by aid agencies and no exit. The new entrants were not only of the traditional type—from new donors such as China, Slovenia, and Thailand—but also of entirely new types—agencies with different approaches to raising or disbursing funds. These new types included the Millennium Challenge Corporation, distributing most of its grants to countries meeting objective standards, and the Global Fund to Fight AIDS, Tuberculosis, and Malaria, focusing on a tight group of cross-border problems. In response to these three trends, the aid industry emphasized "harmonization," the buzzword for trying to coordinate the efforts of different aid agencies.

Reinventing the industry

Looking back from 2030, it is clear that these three trends would force the traditional model of foreign aid to change. The aid industry was steadily transformed from one dominated by a few large agencies to one that was far more competitive and far more subject to competition from such substitutes as bonds, loans from private banks, and private giving.

Traditional development needs also were changing. Good-value loans to governments were not in short supply: as spreads narrowed and credit ratings improved, most developing countries became able to borrow commercially at attractive terms (see chapter 3).

As a result of these changes, more and more aid agencies were supplying fewer and smaller poor countries. To some extent the industry was becoming a victim of its own success: the share of the developing world's population living in extreme poverty had declined by nearly half in just two decades. The population and economic weight of very poor countries had also fallen: with China, India, and Indonesia too well-off to receive subsidies from the International Development Association (IDA), IDA recipients generated less than 1 percent of world GDP in 2030, down from 5 percent in 1970 (figure 1).

In retrospect, the trajectory of the aid industry was already clear by 2005: it was going to be large grants, ever-more-sophisticated technical advice, and harmonization. The grants were preceded by louder and louder calls for a "big push"—for example, in the U.K. government's proposal for an international financing facility and in the much-cited report of the UN Millennium Project (2005). With richer donors and fewer badly struggling countries, the logic was that grants, if aimed well, could buy development. The technical advice was a much quieter

Figure **1** **Poor countries grow, IDA shrinks**

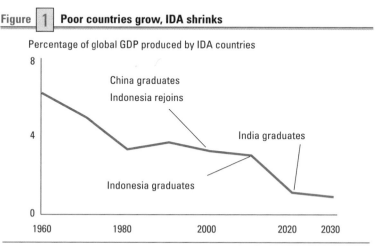

Percentage of global GDP produced by IDA countries

China graduates
Indonesia rejoins

India graduates

Indonesia graduates

1960   1980   2000   2020   2030

Note: Scenarios are not forecasts. The scenario reflected here assumes that the income cutoff for IDA membership does not change and that countries grow at trends slightly (0.33 percent annually) above historical rates.
Source: Historical data from IDA and from World Bank, World Development Indicators database; authors' projections.

success story. The 1970s and 1980s had seen widespread fiscal instability and inflation; by 2005 these blights had been met head-on and subdued by many developing countries. Few people noticed, because as one problem was solved the discussion would move on to the next, such as providing infrastructure or cutting red tape. Finally, harmonization had become an obsession of an increasingly competitive industry by 2005.

2010–20: drowning in the "common pool"

By 2010 the aid industry was attempting to kill two birds with one stone: by delivering large grants through a "common pool" mechanism, the Multilateral Fund for Development, it aimed to scale up the amount of aid delivered while also reducing the costs of a fragmented industry.

The rules of the fund, agreed to by donors in 2009, were designed to maximize grants to directly support recipient government budgets—and also to make negotiations with multiple donors much more efficient. Each developing country presented a development strategy to donors, which could then decide to support the strategy, or not, with grants made through the fund. The fund rules prohibited earmarking and specific conditionality: each donor simply had to decide whether or not to support the development strategy of each recipient. Donors unhappy with how the money was spent simply gave less next year. Few donors sent every penny of aid through the fund, but many sent substantial proportions.

The common pool approach embodied high hopes (Kanbur and Sandler 1999), but difficulties quickly became apparent. The strategy was rooted in the conventional wisdom of the early 21st century: find a developing country with good policies and institutions, send aid, and stand back. It worked well for middle-income countries with mature institutions. But many other countries struggled to use the aid effectively. The trouble was that policies and institutions are changed by large flows of aid—which is exactly what washed over the handful of the poorest countries that met the standards set by donors. For such countries the aid flows had effects similar to those of the well-known "resource curse": manufacturing and agriculture were squeezed by appreciating exchange rates (Foster and Keith 2003). More important, democratic institutions were compromised in the rush for control of the new money (see Djankov, Montalvo, and Reynal-Querol 2004; and Knack 2000). Practitioners became disillusioned with the Multilateral Fund for Development, and some began to comment blackly that promising reformers had been drowned in the common pool.

2020–30: discovering discipline

While the pool system did not deliver what had been hoped for, it represented an important step toward the aid system we enjoy today in 2030. Technical assistance was a case in point: by forbidding grants for specified projects, the pool system prevented the old practice of providing money bundled with technical assistance. But that weakness became a strength: by providing cash rather than technical assistance, the pool system left recipients free to buy their own assistance on the open market rather than accepting whatever ad hoc program was bolted onto a loan. A more professional and competitive market for technical assistance emerged as a result.

The pool system's shortcomings also made it clear what had been missing: trying to minimize the costs of chaotic competition was all very well, but what about trying to maximize the benefits? What was needed was a set of systems to impose discipline on donors, service providers, and recipients alike, making them accountable to one another.

The first step toward such discipline was a shift away from the pool as slush fund: rather than cash, recipients received "service credits" that they used to buy services from official aid agencies and accredited commercial service providers (figure 2). This service credit scheme helped to raise the game of aid agencies and encourage entry by infrastructure providers, consultants, and many others. At the same time it supplied aid in a form that was harder for recipient countries to spend unwisely or corruptly, because service credits were redeemable only with recognized agencies and firms. The scheme, which had seemed implausible when proposed nearly 20 years earlier (Easterly 2002), was much easier to implement with the pool in place.

Figure 2 **The official aid market in 2030**

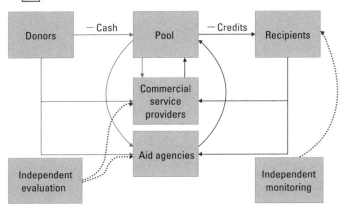

Most important, the service credit scheme cried out for better monitoring and evaluation—a demand that could no longer be ignored. Commercial providers needed to be accredited; aid agencies that delivered services needed to be rated so that credit holders could direct their credits to the most effective;[1] recipients needed to be monitored to assure donors that they were deserving of service credits in the first place. Some donors, skeptical of the credit scheme, used intensive evaluation to justify alternative approaches. A virtuous spiral quickly developed: the service credit scheme strengthened demands for better evaluation, while better evaluation bolstered the case for the service credit scheme (figure 3).

Once the service credit scheme was established, donors were able to experiment with new ideas, giving credits directly to municipalities or even small communities, secure in the knowledge that the system was more and more resistant to waste and abuse. Other donors, armed with the ratings of agencies, felt happy to fund those with a proven track record. But agencies with poor ratings lost funding and struggled to survive.

---

1. An early example was the peer review process launched in the Consultative Group to Assist the Poor (CGAP), where donors reviewed and rated one another (http://www.cgap.org/projects/donor_peer_reviews.html).

Figure 3 **Developing discipline**

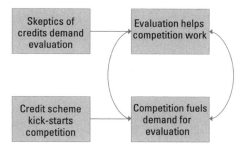

Some aid agencies specialized in service delivery, competing with NGOs and private firms. Others became fund managers on behalf of donors; the best found that they were also able to act on behalf of foundations and charities.

An important side effect was the marginalization of political aid. Clearly outside the loop of service credits, monitoring, and evaluation, aid that was driven by realpolitik became easy to distinguish from aid that was benevolent. (In an early initiative to isolate aid funds from political considerations, the United States set up the Millennium Challenge Corporation in 2002. Its funds were supposed to be disbursed according to objective criteria, and it was scrutinized to see whether it lived up to this promise.) Political aid did not stop, but it shrank—and benevolent aid burgeoned as public suspicion of foreign aid ebbed in rich countries.

Struggling with the big issues in 2030

All this is not to say that the aid industry of 2030 functions perfectly. While many problems have been solved or are being convincingly addressed, others seem intractable, even given the achievements of today's aid system.

The problems are twofold. The first is to address global dangers such as contagious diseases or global warming. The technical work of designing solutions is not hard. What gets in the way is politics. As the world gets richer, countries have the luxury of taking an obstructive stance on one project or another. In 2005 religious and cultural disputes were already undermining global cooperation on HIV/AIDS, though few people foresaw that the disputes would worsen rather than ease. Policy on climate change was even more theological. That such value differences continue to be as important as ever is hardly a surprise.

The second problem is to deal with failed states. Although they have been a hot topic for more than three decades, the international community has yet to formulate an effective response. In many failed states entrepreneurs are scraping out a living by tapping into the laws and institutions of the outside world. But failed states simply do not fit the strictures of the common pool. In the past few years we have seen promising experiments using private firms and NGOs to deliver services while bypassing governments. The hope is that these new approaches will help countries reach a point where the official aid system can help them. But this is speculative. Looking forward to 2050, we can only conclude that if the last of the truly poor are to be helped, the aid industry will have to go through yet another revolution.

PART VI

Conclusion

15

Looking Back, Looking Forward

The modern aid industry, since its birth at the Bretton Woods conference in 1944, has confronted continual change in the context in which it operates—and has continually adapted. More donors now deal with fewer recipients using a far greater array of instruments than in the past. The private sector has emerged as both a substantial source and a major recipient of a bewildering variety of financial flows. And as the world has become richer and more interconnected, loud and sometimes contradictory new demands have arisen for social responsibility and environmental performance. If the aid industry is to continue to adapt to the world's growing complexity, it will have to take advantage of the chaos of competition rather than suppress it.

After World War II the first task was reconstruction. Then came state-led economic development: a broad development agenda was being pursued by governments and supported by government-to-government aid. The Soviet Union's economy was growing strongly, but state-led development efforts elsewhere were less successful. China's Great Leap Forward was a failure that cost millions of lives. The 1960s and 1970s saw a wave of newly independent countries, especially in Africa. Hopes were high as these countries also placed their development plans in the hands of the state, funded by massive levels of foreign debt. Unfortunately, whatever expectations justified the debt buildup were dashed. Only in recent years have borrowers, especially the poorest countries, begun to get debt levels back under control (chapter 3).

The collapse of the Soviet Union strengthened faith in the power of private sector–led growth. The "Washington consensus" in favor of macroeconomic stability, privatization, and deregulation was widely advocated for developing countries. The reason for the consensus was obvious: state-led development had been discredited, the transition economies of Eastern Europe had huge and terribly inefficient state-owned sectors, and the oil shocks, currency collapses, and debt crises of the 1970s and 1980s made basic macroeconomic stability appear to be the sine qua non of good economic performance.

Under the circumstances it was perhaps understandable that other aspects of the Washington consensus—such as establishing and defending property rights and redirecting government money to primary education—were passed by for a few years. As the 1990s came and went, economists began to agree that these things too were important.

Aid agencies respond

Aid agencies have continued to proliferate as the world has changed (chapter 2). After the International Bank for Reconstruction and Development (IBRD), established at Bretton Woods, came the International Development Association and the International Finance Corporation, in response to a perceived need for concessional loans for the poorest countries (IDA) and for finance for private companies operating in developing countries (IFC). Others, such as the African Development Bank, were aimed at the needs of particular regions. Many other aid agencies were set up not because of a clear gap in the capabilities of the industry but because countries or regions were rich enough to join the club of donors, such as Japan and new oil-rich members of the Organization of Petroleum Exporting Countries (OPEC). Since the 1950s new agencies have appeared for all three reasons: because of a new perceived need (Global Fund to Fight AIDS, Tuberculosis, and Malaria), because of new recipients (European Bank for Reconstruction and Development), and because of new donors (China, Slovenia, and Thailand). The reputations of these disparate aid agencies vary, but efforts to measure their performance have so far been rudimentary (chapter 5).

The proliferation of aid agencies creates a challenge for each to find a useful niche, particularly in a world where many recipients are no longer suitable for the traditional lending operations of the World Bank and similar agencies. Some have become, or are becoming, too rich for aid to be appropriate (the Republic of Korea and Taiwan, China, followed by the Czech Republic, Slovenia, Thailand, and others). Others have excellent access to capital markets but millions of poor people in isolated areas who are not fully benefiting (China, India, Mexico). And still others are under such stress that it is hard to know how to give aid effectively (Afghanistan, Haiti, Somalia). Market-rate loans to central governments no longer seem to be the right tool for such cases. The industry is under pressure to respond.

The results of development

There is much to celebrate in world economic performance since 1945. Economic growth has been far higher than predicted at the time (Cooper 2004). Population growth is slowing, and poverty is dramatically down—the share of the world's population living in extreme poverty fell by nearly half between 1981 and 2001. There is no obvious sign that these trends are stopping—2004 saw the highest growth in the developing world since the early 1970s, and trade, foreign investment, and international capital flows have all grown rapidly.

This success has, of course, not been uniform. The East Asian tigers, followed by China, have delivered growth at miraculous levels for decades and appear to have fully recovered from the Asian crisis of 1997. Eastern Europe too, after a rocky start, seems to be moving in the right direction: many of the region's countries have joined the European Union, many are growing quickly, and democracy appears to be well entrenched in the major economies.

Africa presents the big task for the aid industry—plagued by seemingly innumerable problems of economic instability, HIV/AIDS, high trade barriers, weak infrastructure, poor governance, war, and many others. Yet even here there is some hope, as democracies have been established in Nigeria, South Africa, and many smaller countries too.

Elsewhere—the Caspian region, parts of Latin America, the Middle East—new challenges are appearing. Often poverty itself is not the most obvious problem; fragile democracies, failed states, drugs, crime, and terrorism variously afflict different countries in these regions.

Still, the news has on balance been good. The largest countries of all, China and India, may be on their way to claiming status as major powers, and strong growth in both has pulled hundreds of millions of people out of poverty.

The role of the private sector

The success of China, India, and the East Asian tigers, coupled with the failure of the Soviet Union, has helped build a consensus that the private sector is critical. Private firms produce the new jobs and economic growth essential for poverty reduction. If the aim is pro-poor growth (and it is), there is no substitute for bringing a better business climate to places where poor people already live or can easily move.

At the same time there is disappointment with the pure laissez-faire approach. Free trade, sound money, privatization, and deregulation are helpful but not sufficient to promote growth. Economists and development specialists now realize that the market system is more complex than that. The private sector will struggle without supporting institutions, including the protection of property rights (but see chapter 11 for an account of how entrepreneurs can make do in very difficult circumstances). The consensus supports a good investment climate, but defining exactly what that means or how to get there still poses a challenge. Some reforms, such as making it quick and cheap to set up a new business, are relatively simple. Others, such as streamlining bankruptcy and strengthening corporate governance, turn out to be both technically and politically complex.

To add to this complexity, the development industry (and the companies with which organizations such as IFC works) confronts an increasingly long list of demands for better social and environmental standards. These demands come both from Western nongovernmental organizations (NGOs) and from workers, governments, and NGOs in developing countries. The growing demands are not surprising, in part because globalization generates a sense of connection to what is happening elsewhere in the world, and in part too because rich and poor countries alike are getting richer and so demand more than the simple satisfaction of basic needs.

So we should not be too surprised to see a "race to the top," contrary to popular expectations. That is indeed what seems to be happening. Air quality standards in China, Brazil, and Mexico are improving—and that matters, since these countries together account for nearly two-thirds of foreign direct investment into developing countries (Dasgupta and others 2001). The fastest-growing sectors of outward-bound foreign direct investment from the United States are clean ones, not heavy industries (Legrain 2002). But these encouraging trends also pose dilemmas for investors and aid agencies alike: to respond to competing, even conflicting demands is no simple matter (chapter 10).

Something has clearly been working extremely well over the past few decades, relative to historical standards. Yet there are legitimate doubts about whether the aid industry has been terribly effective—and if it has been effective, about whether it has been important (chapters 5 and 7).

More choices

Aid agencies no longer offer the basic package of loans and grants to governments that they did in the 1950s. The range of instruments has expanded to cover concessional loans, dispute resolution, performance-based grants, loans to the private sector, insurance and guarantees for private investors, equity investments in the private sector, loans to subnational governments such as municipalities, and an array of stand-alone technical assistance. The most notable trend in recent times has been a shift from concessional loans to grants, mostly from bilateral agencies but increasingly from multilateral ones (chapter 4). This shift is in part a response to the Heavily Indebted Poor Countries (HIPC) initiative and to concerns that the poorest countries have unsustainable debt levels. All this adds up to a much richer menu of choices for development finance, with more options for sharing risk and more effective operations.

The choices do not end there. There are plenty of options beyond the new offerings of the established aid agencies. We can expect aid agencies to proliferate further, with the new agencies offering innovative new approaches or pursuing new priorities. The private sector can provide sovereign debt at a cost similar to that of official debt, though developing countries appear to prefer the long maturities of official debt (chapter 3). In any case much of the money flowing to poor countries is no longer sovereign debt (chapter 6). Developing countries increasingly rely on lending to the private sector. Even more striking, huge sums of money are flowing as equity rather than debt—foreign direct investment dwarfs most other sources of finance. Remittances from migrant workers are almost as big (bigger, if China is excluded from the data). Even private charitable donations are substantial, at roughly a quarter the size of official aid flows.

The market for aid today

Developing countries today have many advantages compared with those of 30 or 40 years ago, with more market access, better risk sharing instruments to entice capital, and many more choices of loans, equity, and grants. Yet the aid industry is increasingly concerned about the costs of a fragmented industry.

For some countries these costs are illusory. India, for example, has chosen to work with six preferred partner agencies. Some countries prefer to use private capital markets. Others have taken advantage of multilateral lending to restructure their debt portfolios. For these countries choices simply mean opportunities.

But for other countries competition between aid agencies has not brought opportunity. Some "donor darlings" have been swamped with grants, often in the form of dozens or even hundreds of different projects (see Djankov, Montalvo, and Reynal-Querol 2005 for preliminary analysis of how this might reduce the effectiveness of aid). The institutions of such countries may even have been damaged by these aid flows (chapter 7). Fragile and failed states too are likely to make choices that fail to benefit their people—if they have any government to make choices. Here, competition does not seem to have the beneficial effects we would expect.

With some countries graduating from any need for aid and others faltering so badly that it is hard to provide aid, fewer clients are being pursued by more competitors. How do we make the most out of the situation? While many policy approaches have focused on minimizing the costs of competition, we should not forget to try to maximize the benefits.

For a market for aid to work well, we need better information about what works. The response to the Asian tsunami at the end of 2004 showed that there is no lack of willingness to help; what holds back donors, both private and public, is a lack of conviction that the money will be well used. Better evaluation of projects and agencies would help make that case. At least as important, it would improve the quality of the aid we give, by allowing us to do more of what works and less of what does not. Informed choice, exercised by donor governments and individuals, and by recipients, may turn out to be a powerful force for raising the quality of aid. Without information, mere choice will not be enough.

Recently researchers have been asking questions about donor performance and aid effectiveness (chapters 5 and 9). But research has not yet produced some of the results that would really help: credible ratings of aid agencies, measures of the effectiveness of different types of aid, rigorous randomized trials of specific programs. The innovations in evaluation seem to be coming from NGOs or foundations, but these institutions are unlikely to take on the task of evaluating the aid industry.

One thing seems certain, though: with more choices available, taxpayers, private givers, recipients, and others are all going to ask increasingly keen questions about the performance of different aid agencies.

Geopolitics still matters

Crude measures of aid quality suggest that aid allocation is less politically driven today than it was in the late 1980s, and aimed more at the
poor and at countries with good governance (chapter 5). But this
trend can be reversed, and even if it is not, politics will not go away.
Most obviously, the continuing reverberations of the "war on terror"
will shape aid to places such as Afghanistan and Iraq. But less
obvious—and perhaps more important in the long run for the aid
industry—are other geopolitical challenges. There is the drive for
energy security from the West and from new powers such as China
and India. And there is the problem of failed states, possibly provoking peacekeeping operations, war driven by humanitarian concerns,
and attempts to pacify the "white spaces" between governments. This
is a huge development challenge; it is also part of the battle against terrorism, drugs, and infectious diseases. Aid policy and foreign policy
will remain intertwined.

Getting the best out of harmonization and competition

The world is a complicated place politically, socially, and economically.
It is not about to become simpler. The aid industry too is growing more
complex, more fragmented, and more competitive; that, at least, is what
most participants in a recent poll on the future of aid believe, and it is
what we believe too.[1] That is frightening to some, but we should not be
frightened. A simplistic, monolithic aid industry, however "harmonized," cannot deal with a complex world. The challenge is to get the
best out of both harmonization and competition.

In some ways the tension between harmonization and competition
reminds us of the old development debate between "balanced growth"
and "unbalanced growth." Advocates of balanced growth argued for
coordinating infrastructure, education, and complementary industries
in a "big push" to achieve growth. That sounds reasonable, of course—

---

1. For information on the poll, go to http://rru.worldbank.org/Graphs/Future-Aid-Industry.aspx.

the challenge is to make it happen without the big push becoming a big flop. The bigger the push, the bigger the risk.

Unbalanced growth is a chaotic process in which shocks are painful but shake up the established economic order and allow unexpected new businesses to thrive. We are fans of unbalanced growth on the grounds that chaos is what we can expect anyway, and one should work out how to take best advantage of that chaos.

Harmonization, like balanced growth, is appealing but very hard to get right. A competitive aid industry will be chaotic and will always be trying out new things, and in the process aid agencies will make many mistakes. But if the market for aid works well, with rigorous testing of new ideas and a willingness to pull the plug on failures, it will be productive chaos. In fact, freedom to fail should ideally be built into the structure of aid projects and aid contracts.

Imagine a messy world of new experiments and many small failures, overshadowed by the ability of good ideas to flourish. That is a description of any successful economy in the modern world. It could, and should, describe the aid industry too.

References

Chapter 2

Easterly, William. 2002. "The Cartel of Good Intentions." *Foreign Policy* (July–August): 40–49.

Knack, Stephen, and Aminur Rahman. 2004. "Donor Fragmentation and Bureaucratic Quality in Aid Recipients." Policy Research Working Paper 3186. World Bank, Development Research Group, Washington, D.C.

Verleger, P. K. 1993. *Adjusting to Volatile Energy Prices.* Washington, D.C.: Institute for International Economics.

World Bank. 2004. *Global Monitoring Report 2004: Policies and Actions for Achieving the Millennium Development Goals and Related Outcomes.* Washington, D.C.

Chapter 3

IMF (International Monetary Fund). 1999. *International Capital Markets: Developments, Prospects, and Key Policy Issues.* World Economic and Financial Surveys. Washington, D.C. http://www.imf.org/external/pubs/ft/icm/1999/index.htm.

————. 2004. *Global Financial Stability Report.* Washington, D.C. http://www.imf.org/External/Pubs/FT/GFSR/2004/02/index.htm.

Setty, Gautam, and Randall Dodd. 2003. "Credit Rating Agencies: Their Impact on Capital Flows to Developing Countries." Special Policy Report 6. Financial Policy Forum, Washington, D.C.

Chapter 4

World Bank. 2004. *Global Development Finance 2004: Harnessing Cyclical Gains for Development.* Washington, D.C.

Chapter 5

Burnside, Craig, and David Dollar. 2000. "Aid, Policies and Growth." *American Economic Review* 90 (4): 847–68.

Dollar, David, and Victoria Levin. 2004. "The Increasing Selectivity of Foreign Aid, 1984–2002." Policy Research Working Paper 3299. World Bank, Development Research Group, Washington, D.C.

McGillivray, Mark. 1989. "The Allocation of Aid among Developing Countries: A Multi-Donor Analysis Using a Per Capita Aid Index." *World Development* 17 (4): 561–68.

Radelet, Steven. 2003. "Bush and Foreign Aid." *Foreign Affairs* (September–October): 104–17.

Roodman, David. 2004. "An Index of Donor Performance." Working Paper 42. Center for Global Development, Washington, D.C. (Updated annually.)

World Bank. 2003. "Governance Research Indicator Country Snapshot (GRICS): 1996–2002." http://info.worldbank.org/governance/kkz2002/.

————. 2004. *Global Monitoring Report 2004: Policies and Actions for Achieving the Millennium Development Goals and Related Outcomes.* Washington, D.C.

Chapter 6

Adelman, Carol. 2003. "The Privatization of Foreign Aid." *Foreign Affairs* 82 (6): 9–14.

OECD (Organisation for Economic Co-operation and Development). 2003. "Philanthropic Foundations and Development Cooperation." *DAC Journal 2003* 4(3).

————. n.d. "Remittances as Development Finance." http://www.oecd.org/dataoecd/62/17/34306846.pdf.

Radelet, Steven. 2005. Comments in debate, U.S. Aid: Generous or Stingy? Center for Global Development, Washington, D.C., January 13. (Transcript at http://www.cgdev.org/docs/0113aid_debatetranscript.pdf.)

Ratha, Dilip. 2003. "Workers' Remittances." In World Bank, *Global Development Finance 2003: Striving for Stability in Development Finance.* Washington, D.C. http://www.worldbank.org/prospects/gdf2003/.

Chapter 7

Brautigam, Deborah, and Stephen Knack. 2004. "Foreign Aid, Institutions and Governance in Sub-Saharan Africa." *Economic Development and Cultural Change* 52 (2): 255–86.

Brook, Penelope J., and Suzanne M. Smith, eds. 2001. *Contracting for Public Services: Output-Based Aid and Its Applications.* Washington, D.C.: World Bank.

Djankov, Simeon, Jose G. Montalvo, and Marta Reynal-Querol. 2005. "The Curse of Aid." World Bank, Washington, D.C.

Harford, Tim. 2003. "Iraq's Oil Wealth Must Flow Straight to Its People." *Financial Times*, Comment and Analysis, September 26.

Isham, Jonathan, Lant Pritchett, Michael Woolcock, and Gwen Busby. 2003. "The Varieties of Resource Experience." World Bank, Washington, D.C.

Knack, Stephen. 2000. "Aid Dependence and the Quality of Governance: A Cross-Country Empirical Analysis." Policy Research Working Paper 2396. World Bank, Development Research Group, Washington, D.C.

Rajan, Raghuram G., and Arvind Subramanian. 2005. "What Might Prevent Aid from Enhancing Growth?" International Monetary Fund, Washington, D.C.

Sala-i-Martin, Xavier, and Arvind Subramanian. 2003. "Addressing the Natural Resource Curse: An Illustration from Nigeria." IMF Working Paper 03/019. International Monetary Fund, Washington, D.C.

World Bank. 2000. *Can Africa Claim the 21st Century?* New York: Oxford University Press.

Chapter 8

Birdsall, Nancy, Stijn Claessens, and Ishac Diwan. 2003. "Policy Selectivity Forgone: Debt and Donor Behavior in Africa." *World Bank Economic Review* 17 (3): 409–35.

Clements, Benedict, Sanjeev Gupta, Alexander Pivovarsky, and Erwin R. Tiongson. 2004. "Foreign Aid: Grants versus Loans." *Finance and Development*, September, pp. 46–49.

Djankov, Simeon, Jose G. Montalvo, and Marta Reynal-Querol. 2004. "Helping the Poor with Foreign Aid: The Grants vs. Loans Debate." World Bank, Washington, D.C.

IFIAC (International Financial Institution Advisory Commission). 2000. Report submitted to the U.S. Congress and U.S. Department of the Treasury, March 8 (Meltzer report). http://www.house.gov/jec/imf/meltzer.htm.

Odedokun, Matthew. 2004. "Multilateral and Bilateral Loans versus Grants: Issues and Evidence." Special issue, *World Economy* 27 (2): 239–63.

Rogoff, Kenneth. 2004. "The Sisters at 60." *The Economist*, July 22.

Sawada, Yasuyuki, Hirohisa Kohama, and Hisaki Kono. 2004. "Aid, Policies, and Growth: A Further Comment." University of Tokyo, Faculty of Economics.

Chapter 9

Djankov, Simeon, Jose G. Montalvo, and Marta Reynal-Querol. 2004. "Helping the Poor with Foreign Aid: The Grants vs. Loans Debate." World Bank, Washington, D.C.

Odedokun, Matthew. 2003. "Economics and Politics of Official Loans versus Grants." WIDER Discussion Paper 2003/04. World Institute for Development Economics Research, Helsinki.

Rajan, Raghuram G., and Arvind Subramanian. 2005. "What Might Prevent Aid from Enhancing Growth?" International Monetary Fund, Washington, D.C.

Sawada, Yasuyuki, Hirohisa Kohama, and Hisaki Kono. 2004. "Aid, Policies, and Growth: A Further Comment." University of Tokyo, Faculty of Economics.

Sutton, John. 2005. "Competing in Capabilities: An Informal Overview." First Development Economics Lectures, World Bank, Washington, D.C., April 21.

Chapter 10

Ayres, Ian, and John Braithwaite. 1992. *Responsive Regulation: Transcending the Deregulation Debate.* New York: Oxford University Press.

Freeman, Richard B., and Kimberly Ann Elliott. 2003. *Can Labor Standards Improve under Globalization?* Washington, D.C.: Institute for International Economics.

Gordon, Kathryn. 2000. "Rules for the Global Economy: Synergies between Voluntary and Binding Approaches." Working Paper on International Investment 1999/3. Organisation for Economic Co-operation and Development, Directorate for Financial, Fiscal, and Enterprise Affairs, Paris.

Oxford Analytica. 2000. "Corporate Responsibility: Private Sector Initiatives to Promote Socially Responsible Business Practices in Developing Countries." Oxford Analytica Brief. Oxford.

Ward, Halina. 2004. "Public Sector Roles in Strengthening Corporate Social Responsibility: Taking Stock." World Bank and International Finance Corporation, Corporate Social Responsibility Practice, Washington, D.C.

Chapter 11

Omer, Abdusalam. 2003. "Supporting System and Procedures for the Effective Regulation and Monitoring of Somali Remittance Companies (*Hawala*)." United Nations Development Programme, Nairobi.

Somaliland Times. 2004. "Somalia Telecoms Boom without Government." July 22.

United States Institute for Peace. 1998. *Removing Barricades in Somalia: Prospects for Peace.* Washington, D.C.

Chapter 12

Garn, M., Jonathan Isham, and Satu Kahkonen. 2000. "Should We Bet on Private or Public Water Utilities in Cambodia? Evidence on Incentives and Performance from Seven Provincial Towns." World Bank, Washington, D.C.

O'Leary, Declan. 2002. "Output-Based Aid Report: Socioeconomic Profiles and Processes for Four Pilot Towns." Report prepared for the World Bank, Washington, D.C.

————. 2004. "Experiences of an Output-Based Aid (OBA) Approach for Water Supply in Cambodia." Report prepared for the World Bank, Washington, D.C.

Chapter 13

BBC Online. 2004. "Oxfam Offers Chicks for Christmas." October 3. http://news.bbc.co.uk/2/hi/uk_news/3711134.stm.

Djankov, Simeon, Jose G. Montalvo, and Marta Reynal-Querol. 2004. "Helping the Poor with Foreign Aid: The Grants vs. Loans Debate." World Bank, Washington, D.C.

Klein, Michael, and Tim Harford. 2004. "The Global Challenge of Corporate Governance." *Financial Times*, May 3. (Also available at http://www.tim harford.com/writing/2004/05/global-challenge-of-corporate.html.)

OECD (Organisation for Economic Co-operation and Development). 2002. *Trends in International Migration*. Paris. http://www.oecd.org/document/36/ 0,2340,en_2825_494553_2515108_1_1_1_1,00.html.

Ratha, Dilip. 2003. "Workers' Remittances." In World Bank, *Global Development Finance 2003: Striving for Stability in Development Finance*. Washington, D.C. http://www.worldbank.org/prospects/gdf2003/.

Reynolds, Paul. 2004. "Public Opinion Pushes Governments." BBC Online, December 31. http://news.bbc.co.uk/2/hi/asia-pacific/4137867.stm.

Rogerson, Andrew. 2004. "The International Aid System 2005–2010: Forces For and Against Change." ODI Working Paper 235. Overseas Development Institute, London. http://www.odi.org.uk/publications/web_papers/aid _system_rogerson.pdf.

Seabright, Paul. 2004. *The Company of Strangers: A Natural History of Economic Life*. Princeton, N.J.: Princeton University Press.

World Bank. 2004a. *Global Development Finance 2004: Harnessing Cyclical Gains for Development*. Washington, D.C.

———. 2004b. *World Development Report 2004: Making Services Work for Poor People*. New York: Oxford University Press.

Chapter 14

Djankov, Simeon, Jose G. Montalvo, and Marta Reynal-Querol. 2004. "Determinants of Aid Effectiveness." World Bank, Washington, D.C.

Easterly, William. 2002. "The Cartel of Good Intentions." *Foreign Policy* (July–August): 40–49.

Foster, Mick, and Andrew Keith. 2003. "The Case for Increased Aid: Report to the Department for International Development." Overseas Development Institute, London. http://www.odi.org.uk/PPPG/cape/seminars/may04papers/Foster _Case_for_Increased_Aid.pdf.

Kanbur, Ravi, and Todd Sandler. 1999. "The Future of Development Assistance: Common Pools and International Public Goods." Overseas Development Council, Washington, D.C.

Knack, Stephen. 2000. "Aid Dependence and the Quality of Governance: A Cross-Country Empirical Analysis." Policy Research Working Paper 2396. World Bank, Development Research Group, Washington, D.C.

Rogerson, Andrew. 2004. "The International Aid System 2005–2010: Forces For and Against Change." ODI Working Paper 235. Overseas Development Institute, London. http://www.odi.org.uk/publications/web_papers/aid _system_rogerson.pdf.

UN Millennium Project. 2005. *Investing in Development: A Practical Plan to Achieve the Millennium Development Goals.* New York. http://unmp.forum one.com/.

Chapter 15

Cooper, Richard. 2004. "A Half Century of Development." Paper presented at the Annual World Bank Conference on Development Economics, Washington, D.C., May 3–4. http://econ.worldbank.org/abcde/.

Dasgupta, Susmita, Benoit Laplante, Hua Wang, and David Wheeler. 2001. "Confronting the Environmental Kuznets Curve." *Journal of Economic Perspectives* 16 (1): 147–68.

Djankov, Simeon, Jose G. Montalvo, and Marta Reynal-Querol. 2005. "The Effectiveness of Foreign Aid in a Donor Fragmented World." World Bank, Washington, D.C.

Legrain, Phillippe. 2002. *Open World: The Truth about Globalisation.* London: Abacus.

About the Authors

Michael Klein

Michael Klein is vice president for private sector development jointly for the World Bank and the International Finance Corporation as well as chief economist of IFC. Earlier, he was director of the joint World Bank–IFC Private Sector Advisory Services Department, covering advice on investment climate, corporate governance, corporate social responsibility, privatization transactions, and foreign investment. He first joined the World Bank in 1982, but has since worked as chief economist of the Royal Dutch/Shell Group (1997–2000) and as head of the unit for non-OECD economies at the Organisation for Economic Co-operation and Development (1991–93). Before joining the World Bank, Mr. Klein was active in Amnesty International and served on its German board and International Executive Committee. He studied in New Haven and Paris and received his doctorate in economics from the University of Bonn.

Tim Harford

Tim Harford is an economist at the International Finance Corporation, where he has been working on long-term strategy for IFC in the Office of the Chief Economist. Before joining IFC, he was the first Peter Martin Fellow at the *Financial Times,* where he was a leader writer in 2003. His book of popular economics, *The Undercover Economist* (Oxford University Press USA; Little Brown UK), will be published in late 2005. Tim was also an economist and scenario expert at Shell International. He holds an MPhil and a BA from Oxford University.

A Note on the Book

The book was copyedited by Alison Strong; the original graphs were drawn by Carol Levie. The text was typeset in Minion, a typeface designed by Robert Slimbach in 1990 and drawn on classical proportions of old-style typefaces of the Renaissance period. The display typefaces are from the Univers family, designed by Adrian Frutiger in 1957. Naylor Design, Inc., of Washington, D.C., designed the interior pages, Dragan Rockvic drew the cover art, and Benoît Bekaert was the colorist. MasterPrint, Inc., of Newington, Virginia, printed and bound the book, using permanent, acid-free paper.